DAWN OVER OMAN

The Kesra named Oman Mazun
And Mazun, O friend! is a goodly land
A land abounding in fields and groves
With pastures and unfailing springs

                              (PRE-ISLAMIC POET)

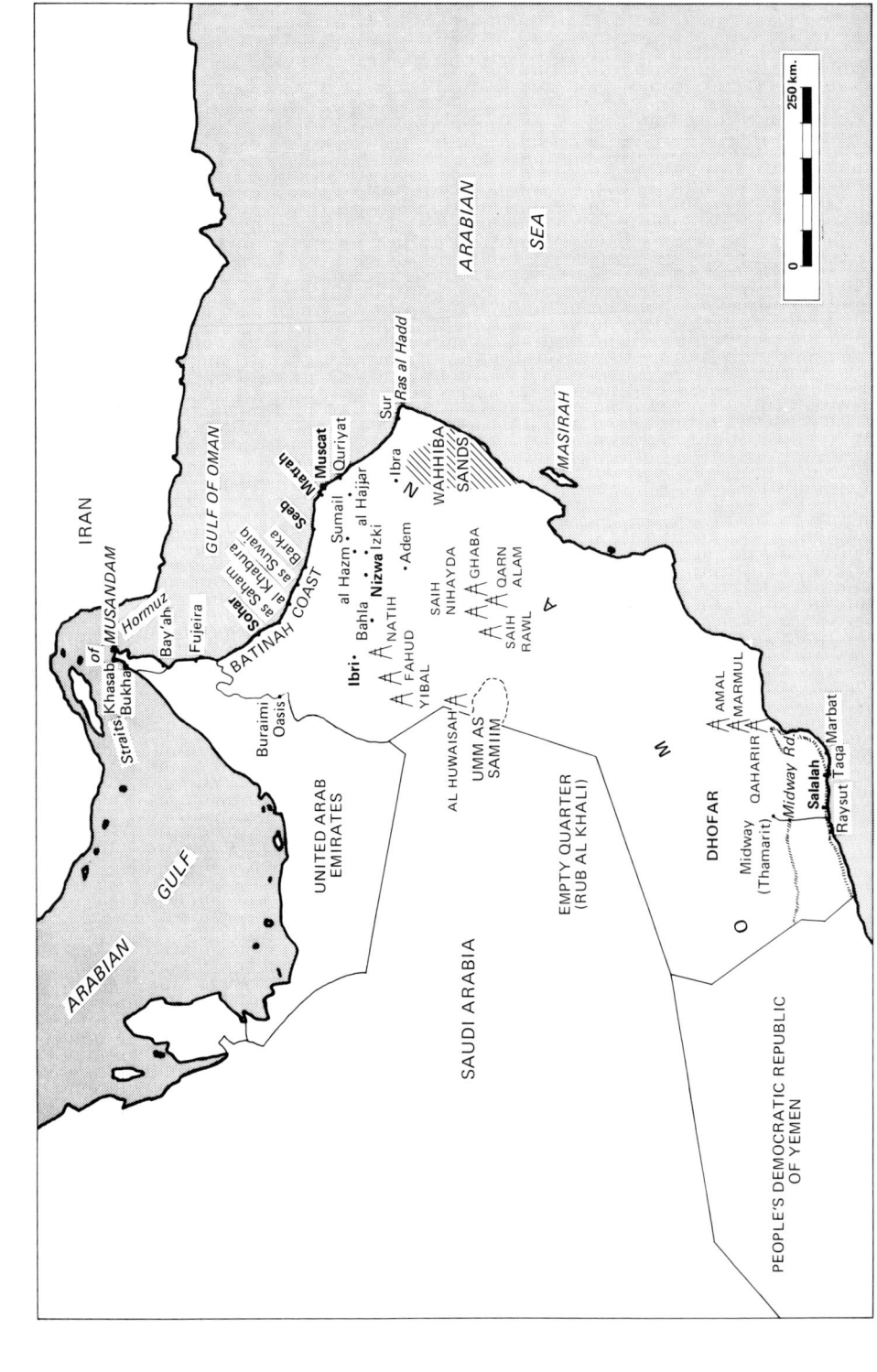

PAULINE SEARLE

DAWN OVER OMAN

London
GEORGE ALLEN & UNWIN
Boston   Sydney

First published in 1975 by Khayat Book and Publishing Co, Beirut
This edition, entirely revised and re-set, 1979

This book is copyright under the Berne Convention. All rights are reserved. Apart from any fair dealing for the purpose of private study, research, criticism or review, as permitted under the Copyright Act, 1956, no part of this publication may be reproduced, stored in a retrieval system, or transmitted, in any form or by any means, electronic, electrical, chemical, mechanical, optical, photocopying, recording or otherwise, without the prior permission of the copyright owner. Enquiries should be sent to the publishers at the undermentioned address:

GEORGE ALLEN & UNWIN LTD
40 Museum Street, London WC1A 1LU

© George Allen & Unwin (Publishers) Ltd, 1979

British Library Cataloguing in Publication Data

Searle, Pauline
  Dawn over Oman. – Revised ed.
  1. Oman – Description and travel
  I. Title
  915.3'5   DS247.062   79-40126

ISBN 0-04-915023-5

Typeset in 11 on 13 point Palatino by Western Printing Services, Bristol and printed in Great Britain by W. &. J. Mackay Ltd, Chatham

Contents

List of Illustrations	*page* xi
Acknowledgements	xiii
Glossary	xv
List of Abbreviations	xix
Introduction	xxi

PART ONE

1.	The Long Night	3
2.	The Pre-Dawn	18

PART TWO

3.	The Background	29
4.	The Desert	41
5.	The Cities	51
6.	The Coastline	65
7.	The Mountains	78
8.	The Northern Peninsula	85
9.	The Southern Province	92

PART THREE

10.	Natural History	105
11.	Arts and Crafts	115

PART FOUR

12.	The Dawn Breaks	127

Bibliography	141
Index	143

Illustrations

1.	Old Matrah	*page*	1
2.	Grave-mounds near Ibri		7
3.	Rock art		9
4.	Falaj, or irrigation channel		11
5.	The round tower of Nizwa fort		21
6.	The main street of Matrah		24
7.	The Bab al Kabir in Muscat		25
8.	Typically dramatic mountain scenery		30
9.	Taking a break in the mountains		33
10.	Sultan Qaboos signing the Participation Agreement		39
11.	The Wahhiba sand-dunes		42
12.	A proud camel-owner		44
13.	An early-morning meeting in the desert		46
14.	Muscat harbour		52
15.	Muscat harbour		53
16.	Sultan Said bin Timur's 'autograph book'		56
17.	Certificate of manumission		58
18.	Matrah from the sea		60
19.	The villages of the Batinah		66
20.	A boum unloads cargo at Sur		74
21.	The hand-carved and painted stern of a dhow		75
22.	Hand-carved doors		76
23.	A familiar Omani scene		80
24.	A track in the interior		81
25.	The track leading to Fahud		83
26.	Musandam from the air		87
27.	Villages in Musandam		89
28.	A Shihuh village		90
29.	A frankincense bush		94
30.	A unit of Firqa troops		99
31.	Gaily dressed women of Salalah		101
32.	An oryx		107
33.	Harvest of the sea		112
34.	Shells discovered in Oman		114
35.	An Omani hurss		119
36.	A traditional silver coffee pot		121

xii Illustrations

37.	A silver khanjar	*page* 122
38.	A young Omani beauty	126
39.	Koranic scholars in class	129
40.	Building development in the Ruwi Valley	137
41.	Sultan Qaboos bin Said	140

Acknowledgements

With thanks to: John Jennings (geology), Rudi Jäckli (rock art), David S. Henderson (oryx), Michael Searle, David Shepherd (ornithology), Dr Donald Bosch (conchology), Anne de Young (missionary work in Oman), Major Shane Lucas (firearms), W. Peyton, the late Andrew Williamson, Richard Carrington, G. Reid-Anderson, Major-General J. D. C. Graham CBE, Brigadier Colin Maxwell, Colonel Malcolm Dennison, Major Peter Sincock, Cyril Cooper MBE, Patsy Wills, John Carter, Douglas Galloway, Julian Paxton, Alastair Aked, Lorens Hedelund, Harvey Staal, Ralph Daly; and especially to:

> Sayyid Fahad bin Mahmood al Said,
> Sheikh Amor Ali Ameir and
> H. E. Hassan Said Mohammed

for their help and cooperation.

Cover picture copyright David S. Henderson, MMPA; photographs 1, 2, 3, 16, 20, 21, 22, 23, 24, 26, 27, 29, 33, 35, 36, 37, 38, 39, 40 courtesy of the Ministry of Information and Culture, Oman, through the good offices of Michael Rice & Co Ltd; photographs 8, 9, 11, 12, 13, 14, 15, 34 by Michael Searle; photographs 4, 5, 6, 7, 18, 19, 28, 31, 41 from the author's own collection; photograph 10 by Julian Paxton; photograph 30 courtesy of the Sultan of Oman's Land Forces; photograph 32 courtesy of the Zoological Society of London; photograph 25 courtesy of Williams Bros Ltd; manumission certificate (17) courtesy of the British Embassy, Muscat.

Sketches by Michael Beeching (prints available through Arabian Art Enterprises, 13–14 New Bond Street, London W1).

Glossary

Abu Ali	Nineteenth-century tribe in Central Oman
Adu	Enemy
Aflaj	Plural of 'falaj' (water channel)
Akkadian period	About 1700 BC
Al Bakr al Wahsh	Literally 'wild cow', a name for the oryx
Al Bu Sa'id	Dynasty to which the present ruler of Oman belongs
Bab al Kabir	Literally 'large gate', usually the main gate of a city
Badawi	Proper name for 'Bedu'
Bait Kathir	Tribe in Southern Oman
Bani Hina	Tribe in Northern Oman
Bani Julandu	Tribe in Northern Oman
Bani Riyam	Tribe in Central Oman
Barasti	Palm-frond dwellings
Bedu	Nomad or desert dweller
Bin Sola	Literally 'son of violence', a name for oryx
Bum	Boat with a beaked prow and sharp stern
Baghala	Large sailing ship with high poop and stern
Burma	Large pot used in the making of rosewater
Dhow	Arabian sailing vessel
Dilmun	Legendary island associated with present-day Bahrain
Dirhams	Currency used in the Gulf area
Dish-dash	All-enveloping white cotton garment worn by men in Oman
Dum dum	Evening gun
Duru	Tribe in Central Oman
Eid al Adha	Feast commemorating the sacrifice of Abraham and characterised by the slaughtering of sheep
Falaj	Water channel
Firqas	Home Guard
Garab	Skin disease affecting camels
the Hadhramaut	Coastal province of South Yemen
Hadhrami	Belonging to the Hadhramaut
Halwa	Sticky sweet found everywhere in the Middle East
Harasis	Tribe in Central Oman
Huri	Canoe from hollowed-out tree-trunk, now with outboard motor
Hurss	Silver box worn on a chain round the neck and usually containing a verse from the Koran
Ibadhis	Ultra-orthodox Moslems belonging to the Kharijite sect

Glossary

Imam	Religious leader
Imamate	Rule of an Imam, or the area controlled by an Imam
Jamdat Nasr period	About 3,000 BC
Janabah	Tribe in Central Oman
Jebel	Mountain
Jebel Akhdar	Literally 'green mountain', a range in Central Oman
Jabalis	Mountain dwellers
Khanjar	Curved dagger peculiar to Oman
Kharijites	Breakaway sect from orthodox Moslems
Khoja	Sect of Shi'ah Moslems
Kitab al Masalik wal-Mamalik	Book written by Istakri between the fourth and tenth centuries
Kohl	Powder, usually antimony, used to darken eyelids and lashes
Kumma	White cloth hat, usually embroidered, worn by men in Oman
Kumzara	Language spoken by the Shihuh in Musandam
Kurss	Copper vessel used in the making of rosewater
Loomi	Lime
Mabkhara	Triangular stand for clothes under which incense is burned
Magan	Legendary kingdom of Arabia
Mahfif	Leather cord worn by Jebalis of South Dhofar round their hair
Majlis	Council or room in which guests are received
Marzuban	Persian governor
Mazun	Possible ancient name for Oman
Mecca	City in Saudia Arabia, the religious centre of Moslems
Medina	Arabic for 'town', also a religious city in Saudia Arabia
Mezoon	See Mazun
Mihrab	Niche or slab in a mosque indicating the direction of Mecca
Minaret	Tower in a mosque from which the muezzin calls the faithful to prayer five times a day
Mosque	Moslem place of worship
Muezzin	Priest who calls the faithful to prayer
Natih	Geological term for certain strata, also an oilfield in Central Oman
Qawasim	Warlike pirates from the Trucial Coast in the eighteenth century
Rim	Large white gazelle
Rub al Khali	Empty quarter
Sahila	Small bowl used in making of rosewater
Sayyid(s)	Lords, a title now adopted by members of the Ruling Family in Oman
Shari'a	Moslem law
Shashas	Boats made from palm fronds
Shemaal	North wind
Shihuh	Mountain dwellers in Musandam

Shi'ites	A sect of Moslems
Suq	Bazaar
Tahr	Wild goat
Ubar	Legendary place-name, the Atlantis of Arabia
Umm an Nar culture	A culture which took its name from an island now in Abu Dhabi
Umm as Samiim	Literally 'mother of salt', salt flats in Western Oman bordering the Empty Quarter
Wadi	Rocky, usually dry, watercourse or river valley
Wahhabis	Warlike tribe or sect of orthodox Moslems from Saudi Arabia
Wahl	Mammal said to inhabit the sandy deserts of Oman
Wali	Local governor
Waliyat	District under a wali
Wasia	Geological term for certain strata
Ya'ariba dynasty	Dynasty in eighteenth century Oman

Abbreviations

ARAMCO	Arabian American Oil Company
BP	British Petroleum
CAT	Civil Action Team
CFP	Compagnie Français de Pétroles
COSOAF	Commanding Officer, Sultan of Oman's Air Force
FMC	Food Machinery Corporation
IPC	Iraq Petroleum Co Ltd
OPEC	Organization of Petroleum Exporting Countries
OAPEC	Organization of Arab Petroleum Exporting Countries
PDO	Petroleum Development (Oman) Ltd
PDRY	People's Democratic Republic of Yemen
SAF	Sultan's Armed Forces
SEP	Surrendered Enemy Personnel (after Dhofar War)
SOAF	Sultan of Oman's Air Force
SOLF	Sultan of Oman's Land Forces (new name for SAF)
SON	Sultan of Oman's Navy
UNESCO	United Nation's Educational, Scientific and Cultural Organization

Introduction

Until mid-1970 Oman was among the least known countries in the world. Geographically isolated by the Arabian Sea to the east, the Empty Quarter to the west and mountains to north and south, ruled over by a backward-looking and autocratic Sultan and with no apparent resources, Oman could have remained this way indefinitely. But the discovery of oil was to change everything.

Today Oman is a country ruled over by a progressive young Sultan, and is a member of the Arab League and the United Nations. Ministers fly around the world conferring on political matters; buildings rise overnight; an international airport handles the largest jets and traffic drives bumper to bumper in the area surrounding the capital city, Muscat.

Drive off the main highway, however, and onto the dirt roads and once again one can be in the unchanging Oman of the past, the Oman where warring tribesmen fought and died, where mud forts dominate every likely vantage-point and where inhabitants of oasis towns live as they have done for centuries past.

Every small boy is a miniature warrior and men of every age carry rifles and khanjars, the silver dagger in the ornate sheath that has become the symbol of Oman itself. Festooned with his armoury and his belts of ammunition, the Omani warrior is a proud sight. His traditions of hospitality are pure Bedu and limitless and he is by and large friendly and helpful to travellers, even to those whose manners probably appal him.

Oman still guards its secrets closely. There are few reliable records to be found regarding its history and tribal customs and much of the information the traveller culls is pure conjecture on the part of enthusiastic amateurs. Only in these last few years have archaeologists and other experts been allowed to penetrate the interior and roam comparatively freely. Seeking information is a frustrating business, due largely to the innate politeness and friendliness of the Omani himself, who only wants to help and will agree to any explanation if he feels it is the one the traveller wants to hear.

Oman is full of mysteries – the round stone grave-mounds topping the mountains, the fossil shells hundreds of miles into the desert, the hollow geodes whose origin puzzles even the geologists, and stone implements and potsherds found in the most unexpected places. The average traveller is mystified not least by the multitude of explanations given by so-called experts. He finally gives up to be left with only the wonder of it all.

Yet inroads have been made in the archaeological field and experts have already unearthed enough material to encourage more efforts in the future. Romantics already see Oman as the legendary kingdom of Magan, as part of old Dilmun or the site of the copper mines of King Solomon. Even, who knows, the site of Ubar, the Atlantis of Arabia and a marble city of fabulous riches. Time will tell.

PART 1

1. Old Matrah in the eighteenth century

1. *The Long Night*

To understand the Omani of today and his pride in his country and its development, it is necessary certainly to know something of the past history of Oman but not perhaps too much.

Much has been written about the old Oman – the warring tribesmen, the feuds, the backwardness of the country until as recently as 1970. It has been a journalist's dream to write about these things and to romanticise them. Yet it is as well to remember that during much of this time Western countries, too, had their own sophisticated forms of barbarity; the slave trade after all was perpetrated by those who should have known better, and the worst atrocities ever committed in Oman were almost certainly those committed by the Portuguese.

All things considered the Omanis have come out of it all extremely well. They are among the friendliest people to be found anywhere today and the onrush of civilisation has neither spoiled them nor made them over-suspicious in spite of their monumental efforts to be good Arabs and toe the party line. But they are bored with hearing about the old days and would much rather talk about the recent tempestuous years after the butterfly emerged from the chrysalis and made its first ecstatic flight.

It is necessary to know something of the past, yes, but not to dwell on it hugely.

I remember vividly one night, it must have been in 1968, when I dined in Muscat for the first time. It was dark and we were ready to sit down to dinner when our host pulled back the curtain and beckoned me out onto the balcony of the British Bank of the Middle East, which is situated just outside the city walls and the Bab al Kabir, the main gate of the city. As we stepped out into the darkness a roar of gunfire sounded and we saw in the distance over the harbour a red flash outlining the battlements of Fort Mirani, black against the night sky.

Our host pointed to the gate. Slowly it was beginning to close – we could even hear the rusty hinges and the bolts being drawn. I was transported back to the Middle Ages, even more so later when we crept round the narrow streets with our oil lamps and were joined by Sayyid Abbas bin Feisal, uncle to the Sultan, and one of the few Omanis at that time who mixed freely with the foreigners.

Such was Muscat until 1970 where every night, three hours after sunset or dum dum (the Indian influence was very strong), the guns roared out from the Fort and the gate closed. It was ludicrous but enchanting.

And this was only the top of the iceberg, the part that was visible. Beneath the surface Muscat and the whole of Oman seethed and chafed under the restrictions imposed by their autocratic Sultan, Said bin Timur, a Sultan who lived away down in Salalah, 700 miles across the desert, and who had not even visited his capital for ten years. The whole country was an incredible anachronism.

All that is changed now. Oman's ministers now attend summit conferences and take an increasing part not only in their own but in world affairs. It is a thriving nation with a healthy economy, respected by her neighbours and feared by her enemies, few though they may be. Schools and hospitals flourish, new ports, airports, hotels and housing estates blossom overnight and the Government and the Armed Forces have expanded out of all recognition from that year, so very little time ago.

To chart Oman's progress on a graph would perhaps give the greatest impact, for the ups and downs of history, alternating with long periods of virtual stagnation, would provide very mild variations compared with the vast upswing of the last few years.

The known history of ancient Oman is somewhat sketchy. Certainly many fascinating references occur in various reports and sagas, chiefly from the time of the Portuguese occupation when the subject matter is bloodthirsty in the extreme. It was said at one stage in Oman's chequered career that not a man or boy there died a natural death, and it was probably not far from the truth.

The barbarities practised by the Portuguese overlords in Oman make some of today's war-crimes look like the play of children, but one should see in perspective the brutality practised against slaves who frequently had hands and feet and, more often, noses and ears, cut off for comparatively trivial offences: it was a barbaric area and they were barbaric times.

As to the country itself, many descriptions of Oman and its geography have been passed down to us by passing travellers or sailors who stayed a while and sailed away. As such, they are often suspect from a historical point of view, being highly exaggerated by men unused to lands other than their own and therefore prone to a great wonder.

The prehistory of Oman was virtually unknown until interest became aroused among amateur historians and archaeologists resident in the country with the formation of the Oman Historical Society in 1971. The Society was founded under the guidance of the newly formed Department of Information and Tourism and under the patronage of His Majesty Sultan Qaboos bin Said in an endeavour to salvage as much as possible of the old Oman before it disappeared in the maelstrom of new building and reorganisation that was taking place, and before the new, brash, businesslike Oman lost for ever the atmosphere and surroundings that give it that infinite charm and attraction for local residents and foreigners alike.

Information began accumulating rapidly and from random notes by enthusiastic amateurs and occasional help from visiting professionals new profiles of old Oman began to emerge.

The oldest information, historically, came from an army colonel (now Brigadier Colin Maxwell) who had specialised in collecting flints while on duty down in South Dhofar. Some of these flints were found to rank among the finest Stone Age relics in the world, probably dating from the end of the period 5,000 – 3,000 BC. The flints were sophisticated for the time: leaf-shaped with hundreds of tiny facets formed by exerting great pressure on the flint whilst it was held rigid. From the high quality of the flint outcrop it was assumed that the interior of Dhofar was an important area in this later Stone Age. No remains were found relating to the Old Stone Age but work was hindered by the war. Now the war in Dhofar is over, much worthwhile material will no doubt come to light.

Over the last six years Oman has become a focal point for many archaeologists, geologists and anthropologists. Results have been published and reports correlated and an astonishing amount of material has been amassed in all fields.

Among the first of the experts to arrive in Oman with offical blessing was a Danish archaeological team, which visited the country for four months in 1973 at the invitation of the Government, who financed the expedition on the understanding that all finds belonged to Oman and that the team should publish the results of their work.

The team of five archaeologists from the Moesgaard Museum of Pre-History at Aarhus spent most of their time exploring an old trade route from Buraimi Oasis in the north running eastwards to Sohar on the Batinah coast of Oman and the fertile area around Ibri between the mountains of the interior and the desert. The principal interest for the archaeologists lay in the 'grave-mounds' which have puzzled travellers in Oman for many years. About a hundred of these graves were examined and, although they had been robbed of their contents, there were remains of fine painted pottery and incised stone vessels testifying to the sophistication of the civilisation of the time.

The grave-mounds themselves were beehive-shaped and made of impressive masonry. They were well planned and up to four metres (13 feet) high and ten metres (33 feet) across at the base. The pottery and stone vessels excavated from the graves showed definite connections with those in southern Persia in the fourth millennium BC and with the Jamdat Nasr period of Mesopotamia around 3,000 BC.

The groups of graves appeared to belong to the Umm An Nar culture, named after the island where it was first found by a previous archaeological team in Abu Dhabi, and could support the suggestion that Oman might once have been part of the legendary land of Magan mentioned in cuneiform tablets from about 2,000 BC as trading copper to Mesopotamia. The origin of Magan, or Makan as it is often called, has always been in doubt. Here then was the probability that it was located in Northern Oman and this probability was further supported the following year when substantial copper deposits were found in the area by a mineral research company. In Professor Kramer's translation of tablets from the legendary island of Dilmun, now identified with Bahrain, occurs the blessing 'May the land Magan bring you mighty copper . . .'. Diorite, an igneous rock consisting chiefly of feldspar and hornblende, was also a product of Magan.

2. Beehive-shaped grave-mounds near Ibri in Northern Oman, investigated by the Danish archaeological team in 1973

Since the first official Expedition in 1973 many other expeditions under British, Americans, French, Danes and Italians have visited Oman to explore archaeological sites, study architecture or report on mining and tribal law, water resources and human behaviour. Oman has been dragged, like it or not, under the microscope. Most of the findings have been reported in great detail in volumes I and II of the *Journal of Oman Studies*, published by the Ministry of Information and Culture, Sultanate of Oman, and, while most are interesting enough in their own right, their greatest value probably lies in providing a basis for more detailed future work.

One particular field, peculiar to Oman which proved of great interest to both amateurs and professionals alike is so-called 'rock art'. Many travellers had noticed these usually crude drawings and writings on limestone faces in various parts of the country but, until the arrival of a young British anthropologist, Christopher Clarke, no serious work had been done on the subject.

Clarke spent a few months in 1973 drawing, photographing and mapping some of these drawings and much fascinating data came to light as a result. Only limestone faces were used, and the areas were generally in wadis used by regular travellers over the years, principally in the Wadi Uday between Ruwi and the Saih Hatat or Wadi Bani Kharus just above Awabi or in the Wadi Sahtan near Tabaqa. The areas probably corresponded to camping sites frequented by travellers from the coast to the interior centres of population.

The figures themselves were of particular interest and included not only human figures, generally of the 'stick-man' variety, but animals such as horses, camels, dogs, birds, bulls, ibex and even elephants. Men are represented standing on horses, carrying weapons, often naked or with a simple wrap-around phallus sheath. These figures resembled figures on cylinder seals of the Akkaddian period (about 1700 BC). Some of these figures had obviously served as targets for sling shots and soft lead bullets but this firing probably came later – it seems unlikely that the drawings were made for this purpose.

Non-figurative designs are also common, some simple but others in complicated geometric patterns, while other limestone surfaces bear writing, the texts mainly Koranic. One inscription was found to be in Old South Arabian, the first ever example of pre-Islamic script to be found in Oman outside Dhofar.

The rock drawings and writings have not so far been dated and this dating will be difficult. Many are obviously modern, showing pictures of cars and trucks, while others are also modern but have been copied from the old. However, regarding the pictures in the context of their surroundings and other finds nearby may help to fix a date. Further work on this subject was

3. Typical rock art designs on the limestone face of a wadi in Central Oman

done in the spring of 1973 by Christopher Clarke and Keith Preston. (See 'An Introduction to the Anthropomorphic Content of Rock Art of the Jebel Akhdar' by Keith Preston; *Journal of Oman Studies*, volume II.)

Another fascinating feature to the traveller in Oman is the preponderance of 'falajs' or mud-walled water channels, a form of irrigation introduced by the early Persian settlers which is so efficient that it is still in use today, some two thousand years later. A source of water is located, usually in the foothills of a mountainous area, and the water channelled from here underground to the area to be irrigated. Vertical shafts are dug along the path of the underground channel and connected by a tunnel. Where the watercourse crosses a wadi bed an inverted siphon is used, and on the surface the water is channelled to the various areas by the open ditches.

It is a complicated but eminently successful system and ensures running water throughout the driest summer. Due to this falaj system Oman, in spite of its extremely low rainfall, does not have a great water problem. Certainly at one time the country was fertile and agricultural and there seems little reason why much of it should not be so again.

Whole chapters could be devoted to 'falaj law' whereby villages or individuals are allotted certain times for obtaining water. The arguments relating to the distribution of such water supplies are among the chief subjects raised before the wali in the local majlis, the equivalent of a court of law.

The first conquest of Oman by the Persians, who were to play such a large part in the civilisation of the country, came in 536 BC during the reign of Cyrus the Great. The country at that time appears to have been known as Mazun or Mezoon and was called 'a goodly land, a land abounding in fields and groves with pastures and unfailing springs'. It is interesting to note the similarity between the names Makan or Magan and Mazun and to read that in a battle on the plains near Nizwa a certain Malik defeated the Persian army of 30,000, his sons personally slaying one of the large Persian elephants. It is not so surprising after all to find elephants among the rock drawings.

Perhaps, indeed, some of the stranger animal designs can be explained by the following description of another battle against Persians this time in Syria – 'In order to make up the deficiency under which the Muslim army laboured from want of elephants Qa'qa had recourse to a very ingenious device. He had some camels enveloped in fantastic housings and covered their heads with flowing vestments which gave them a weird and frightful appearance. On whichever side these artificial mammoths went the horses of the Persians shied and got out of control . . .' which was hardly surprising!

4. Open falaj, or irrigation channel, with mud walls crossing a valley in the Jebel Akhdar in Central Oman

Oman was one of the earliest countries to embrace Islam and after the murder of Caliph Othman in AD 656 the 'Kharijites' broke away from the main body of Islam and turned against Ali, the fourth Caliph. The vast majority of the inhabitants of the interior of Oman today are Ibadhis belonging to this group, a very orthodox sect. They do not, however, regard themselves as a breakaway sect, rather as keepers of the true Moslem faith. Their leader is called an 'Imam' and is elected by a council of elders and he is expected to govern uprightly and uphold the true faith and the Shari'a or Moslem law.

The dominant feature of Oman has always been its tribal structure coupled with its geographical isolation. These factors produced an isolationist tribal society still present today in interior Oman. There traditions die hard and so-called civilisation is taken only at its face value. Traditional Bedu hospitality and the old laws are still paramount, and the language spoken is unadulterated and therefore the purest Arabic spoken anywhere today. These are the advantages of such a society.

The disadvantages of such a powerful individualistic way of life are the prevalence of internal strife and tribal differences occasioned by the belief that every man, every tribe is as good as any other – a God-given and admirable creed but, human nature being as it is, not one conducive to unity of purpose. While the Imam by the very nature of his job was capable of uniting the tribes to fight against foreign domination or outside interference, the tribes, left in peace, would tend to fight each other and were in a constant state of rivalry and antagonism. This has its parallel in the fiercely independent attitudes of the Arab nations today, which only statesmen of the calibre of Nasser or Sadat have been able to overcome, and then only for a time.

The first Ibadhi Imam was elected in AD 751, but ruled only four years before he was put to death by troops of the Abbasid Caliph in an attempt to bring Oman under the domination of Baghdad. Years of depravity and confusion followed, but when the famous Caliph Harun ar-Rashid became ruler of the Moslem empire the Omanis were able to shed the yoke of foreign domination and elect their second Imam. By the year AD 996 some sixteen Imams had been elected and foreign intervention had ended. The Imam was still elected by the people and there was no question at this time of natural succession or nepotism.

Another dominant factor in the history of Oman has been the sea. Before the tenth century, Omani shipbuilders were known all over the world for the fineness of their work, and by the early nineteenth century – its heyday – the Omani navy comprised seveny-five ships of the line.

By the tenth century, the town of Sohar on the north of the Batinah coast was at its zenith and has been variously described by historians of the time as 'one of the most splendid cities of the Islamic world', 'the emporium of the whole world', 'one of the greatest seaports of Islam', 'the finest town on the sea of Persia'.

Sohar was the seat of the Marzuban, the Persian Governor, and it was here that the first Moslem delegation came to convert Oman to Islam. By the fourteenth century, however, Sohar was alleged to be a town in ruins and the beautiful houses of bricks, mortar and teak wood were just so much rubble.

By the beginning of the fifteenth century the Eastern Roman Empire collapsed when the Ottoman Turks captured Constantinople and Portugal was forced to divert her thriving spice trade from the Red Sea route to the long route around the Cape of Good Hope. Christians at this time were discouraged from using the Red Sea area at all under threat of death.

The first Portuguese under Vasco da Gama to use the Cape route in 1498 found Omanis occupying settlements all along the East African coast. In the next twenty years, under the notorious Admiral Alfonso d'Albuquerque, the Portuguese established themselves on Omani territory on both the East African coast and the shores of Oman itself. They built forts, including Fort Mirani in Muscat, and their rule was one of almost unmitigated atrocities and brutality. The 150 years of Portuguese domination on these coasts must surely rank among the most brutal occupations in the world's history.

By the mid-seventeenth century their power was on the wane and in 1622, after losing Hormuz in the north to Britain and Persia, they fortified the town of Muscat by building forts on the nearby mountain tops to cover the passes into the city. Many of these forts can still be seen today. They also reinforced the Fort of Jalali, which had been built by the Persians in 1589, at the same time building Fort Mirani. These two forts at either point of the horseshoe harbour give Muscat its distinctive character. Outside Fort Mirani was an area used to execute prisoners sentenced to death which was in use well into this century while nearby, in an open space near the landing now known as the Khor jetty, was the site of the old slave-market.

Meanwhile at Rostaq in the interior of Oman, a new Imam called Nasir bin Murshid had been elected, a man stronger than the usual run of Imams who were in the main largely spiritual leaders. Under Nasir and his cousin, Sultan bin Saif, the Portuguese were finally expelled not only from Oman but from Zanzibar and all the ports north of the Mozambique channel.

Upon his death Sultan bin Saif had ordered that his son,

Balarab bin Sultan, succeed him as Imam and it was Balarab who built the famous fort at Jabrine near Bahla in the interior, one of the strongest and most decorative forts to be seen in Oman. Fort Jabrine took about thirteen years to build and is famous today for its painted ceilings, wood carvings and decorative panels. So beautiful and unusual are the ceilings of Jabrine that in 1971 Sultan Qaboos ordered that an expert be brought to Oman from Britain to view the fort and advise on its preservation. This work has become the special care of the Historical Society, who have themselves reported fully on the present condition of the fort.

Balarab was succeeded by his brother Saif, who ruled until 1711, and it was during Saif's reign that Omani sea power reached its height and Omani sailors became known the world over. War against the Portuguese and their possessions in India continued incessantly during this time but there was comparative peace at home – unusual indeed for Oman.

This period, the Ya'ariba period, saw for the first time unity among the people of Oman and interest in affairs outside the tribal differences that had plagued her so long. Trade flourished and successful expeditions were sent to Malabar and Basra. It also saw the Imamate established as a hereditary appointment, a fact that was to change the dynasty from the Ya'ariba to the Sa'id when the natural successor, Saif bin Sultan II, only twelve years old at the time he should have succeeded, was deemed too young for the appointment.

Ahmad bin Sa'id, the first Imam of the Al Bu Sa'id dynasty, continued to expand trade and finance expeditions outside Oman's shores. His chief problems were the warlike Qawasim of the Trucial coast but he also had troubles within his own family, particularly with his two rebel sons, Saif and Sultan. In 1780 they took over Birka, on the Batinah coast, and the following year went as far as to annex the notorious fort of Jalali in Muscat, staying there for over a year.

Imam Ahmad, whose ideas on patriotism, justice and liberty had earned him a lasting reputation, died in 1783 and his second son, Sa'id, was elected to succeed him, his eldest son, Hilal, having the misfortune to be born blind. Sa'id proved a poor choice and was soon succeeded by his own son, Hamad, though he continued to reside at Rostaq, keeping the title of 'Imam', while Hamad took up residence in Muscat, at this time a thriving entrepôt between the Persian Gulf, India and the Red Sea.

In 1781, French privateers captured a frigate of the Omani navy off Sohar on the north Batinah coast. Hamad promptly captured one of the privateers foolish enough to venture into Muscat, and placed the crew under arrest. Nine years later the French Government sent Hamad another ship in exchange for the captured frigate which was accepted with great jubilation. In her first tussle with 'Western Imperialism' since expelling the Portuguese, albeit on a piratical level, Oman's dignity and independence had been upheld.

Hamad died in 1792 and two other sons of Ahmed, Qais and Sultan, squabbled over the inheritance before coming to a compromise. For the first time the job of ruling the country was divided, Imam Sa'id continuing as the religious leader in Rostaq, Qais retaining Sohar and Sultan governing in Muscat and Birka and keeping political control.

In 1798, during the time of the French Revolution, Oman signed her first political agreement with Britain aimed at excluding French ships from Omani waters and encouraging the establishment of a factory for the East India Company at Bandar Abbas on the Persian coast, then a dependency of Oman. It was the beginning of British-Omani ties which have lasted in varying degrees and through various turmoils until the present day.

In 1804 Sultan Said bin Sultan, 'Said the Great' as he came to be known, came to power in Muscat. He was to reign for over fifty years and see Oman rise to its greatest heights yet. Freed from problems on the home front (the Qawasim from the Trucial States had been subdued and the Wahhabis were temporarily quiet), Sultan Said was able to expand his influence overseas. In 1828 he operated against Bahrain successfully and in the following year he took Dhofar, the 'Frankincense country, mountainous and forbidding, wrapped in thick clouds of fog'.

Early in his reign the death occurred of Imam Sa'id in Rostaq. No replacement was deemed necessary but the sons of Imam Ahmad took to themselves the title of 'Sayyids' or 'Lords', which title was used in the ruling house from then on, the title of 'Imam' lapsing for the time being.

Sultan Said could be said to be the first ruler of Oman who looked outside his own country and extended its prestige outside its normal sphere of influence. He agreed to accept a British resident in Muscat, a 'gentleman of respectability to act as Agent on the part of the Honourable Company in order that no opportunity may be offered to designing men, who are ever eager to promote dissention, and that the friendship of the two states may remain unshook to the end of time, till the sun and moon have finished their revolving career . . .'. Noble words, as applicable today as they were nearly two hundred years ago!

He talked at length with American sailors and merchants and the idea grew of a possible treaty with the United States of America. One Edmund Roberts from Salem, Massachussetts, helped to make his dream a reality and a Treaty of Amity and Commerce was finally concluded in 1833 due largely to Roberts' efforts. The treaty, which accorded various advantages to American merchantmen trading in the areas of Muscat and Zanzibar, was ratified the following year by the USA and Roberts returned to Muscat as a special agent aboard the *Peacock* to exchange documents. In accordance with the treaty American consuls were named for both Zanzibar and Muscat the first of which, Richard Waters, also of Salem, took up his post in Zanzibar in March 1837.

But this was not enough and Sultan Said decided to send a vessel of his own to the United States for, surely, he reasoned, such contracts would prove profitable and increase his own country's status.

In 1840 a somewhat battered barque appeared unannounced in the New York River. To the astonishment of the Port Authorities the barque was found to be commanded by one Al Haj Ahmad bin Na'man, a representative of Sultan Said of Muscat, a place that few people in America had even heard of. Technically she was commanded by an Englishman, William Sleeman, who had brought her from Muscat to New York via St Helena and the passengers included two Englishwomen, one the wife of a trader and the other her personal maid.

For nearly three months Ahmad and his crew stayed on in the United States. Their mission was not official and they saw no-one of any great importance though they did exchange gifts with President Van Buren. But their popularity was great and, as a public relations effort, the mission could be said to have been a resounding success.

In Oman, however, family revolts were growing, particularly during Sultan Said's periodic visits abroad and further incursions from the Wahhabis forced Said to keep garrisons in the towns of Sumail, Izki, Nizwa and Bahla.

After Said's death the empire was divided, the East African possessions going to his son, Majid, and Oman proper to another son, Thuwaini. From this time forth, through a succession of unhappy rulers, Oman's influence was on the decline. The opening of the Suez canal, steam taking the place of sail on the high seas and the measures taken against the slave trade all conspired to unsettle the country and reduce her power. Muscat was still the capital city but influence was fast returning to the isolated and xenophobic interior.

In the year 1915, at Bait al Falaj near Muscat, Sultan Taimur bin Feisal, with British and Indian help, defeated some 3,000 rebel tribesmen from the interior two years after the Sultan's garrisons had been expelled from Nizwa, Izki and Sumail.

In 1920 an agreement was signed at Seeb on the Batinah coast between the Sultan and the principal dissidents from the interior under Isa bin Salih in which the Sultan agreed to peace with the tribes on the understanding that he did not interfere in their internal affairs.

In 1932 Sultan Taimur, then in India, abdicated in favour of his son, Said, who was then twenty-one years old. Said's appointment was recognised by both Britain and the USA, and Oman entered into a comparatively peaceful though materially unproductive period of its history, a period of disputes of a minor order and a period which was to herald in the new Oman on a tide of oil.

The first of these disputes involved the Buraimi Oasis.

2. The Pre-Dawn

There is nothing particular to distinguish the Buraimi oasis from any other in Oman or the neighbouring countries. Spread over several square kilometres, it covers the borders between Oman, Saudi Arabia and Abu Dhabi. Throughout the years Buraimi had been a bone of contention between various tribal factions notably the Wahhabis, a warlike tribe originating in the Nejd who, after nearly seventy years of laying claim to the oasis, finally evacuated it in 1869 only to renew their claim eighty-four years later.

In this type of country frontiers mean little enough under normal conditions – one clump of palm trees or one sand dune being much like another. Tribesmen come and go across the so-called borders all the time and the Buraimi squabble might have gone on indefinitely in this desultory fashion had it not been for the discovery of oil in Qatar in 1949, which gave the contenders something to think about. Saudi Arabia, the most oil-orientated of her neighbours, with an eye to future exploration, promptly pushed her own claim to sovereignty over the otherwise useless oasis and the fight was on. A three-cornered contest naturally developed between oil exploration parties, Aramco and IPC constantly finding themselves in territorial disagreements, pushed no doubt on occasion by their respective governments and personal loyalties.

The British meanwhile were trying to press Sultan Said bin Timur of Oman to take firm action in Buraimi before it was too late, but the proud and autocratic Sultan would brook no advice or countenance any outside interference in the government of his country. This 'laissez faire' attitude naturally encouraged the Saudis and in 1952 they sent a small military unit of some forty soldiers to occupy an area near the village of Buraimi. This at last stirred Sultan Said to action and a joint expedition of Trucial Oman Scouts from Abu Dhabi and the Sultan's Armed Forces from Oman started to march on Buraimi to confront the Saudis. Before they even joined forces, however, a directive from Whitehall halted the expedition and the Omanis, by this time roused to a fever pitch of excitement, were tamely dispersed, puzzled and disillusioned. The outside world needless to say received the impression that the Saudis must have right on their side – a bloodless victory if ever there was one.

Oman had temporarily lost its chance and was forced to go to arbitration. An agreement was signed in Jeddah in 1954 stating that all sides were to withdraw their forces to undisputed territory, replacing them with small police groups of up to fifteen men each. In this way Saudi Arabia established her own right to a slice of the cake and was thereafter able to smuggle in arms and ammunition and bribe the local sheikhs with money and arms.

In 1955 Oman, backed by the British, decided that things had gone far enough and, together with the Trucial Oman Scouts, the Sultan's Armed Forces marched on the Saudi post and forced the Saudi police commander to surrender which he did, together with his fifteen men. But the damage had been done, for during their time of occupation of part of the Buraimi oasis, Saudi Arabia had extended its influence to include tribesmen from the interior of Oman, many of whom still swore allegiance to the Imam in Nizwa rather than to Sultan Said.

In 1954 Imam Mohammed, a respected figure to the end, died in Nizwa and was succeeded by one Ghalib bin Ali of the Bani Hina tribe. Ghalib had a younger brother, Talib, and between the two men the so-called 'Imam's Armed Forces' was formed, with Talib as the commander. By the end of 1955 rebellion proper had broken out in Oman and once again reinforcements were rushed to Buraimi. Britain's enemies had a field day blaming 'imperialist aggression' and even America, who should have known better, echoed the cries of the pack. The Suez crisis which followed only months later did nothing to help.

In October 1954 Ghalib and Talib, the 'terrible twins', had established their rallying point at Bahla, west of Nizwa, with the first intention of throwing the Sultan's forces out of Ibri where the latter had a military post. Their attempt was unsuccessful and they fell back on Nizwa, concentrating their main efforts on propaganda abroad and rallying outsiders to their cause.

It was to take Sultan Said and his army until 1959 finally to defeat the brothers, which he did largely with British help and equipment. The final showdown in the War of the Jebel Akhdar, as it came to be known, took place at Firq, near Nizwa, after much harm had been caused to innocent villagers by both sides. By the end of 1959 Ghalib together with Talib had fled the country, still calling himself the Imam and Ruler of Oman, and occasionally surprising everyone by issuing passports and even postage stamps purporting to come from the Sultanate. There were no more serious threats from Central Oman.

There are still officers and men in the Sultan's Armed Forces today who remember the Jebel Akhdar War with nostalgia and what can only be called affection. The highlight of the war – the capture of the old circular fort of Nizwa – must have been one of the last battles to be fought in the old style with tribesmen waving khanjars, shooting with old muskets and even firing cannon-balls, while out-of-date planes of the Sultan's Air Force attacked the fort, doing remarkably little damage to the three-foot-thick mud walls. One wonders who enjoyed it all the most. To the British officers in the Sultan's Forces it was going back a century or more to the glorious days of Empire when half the world was coloured pink. To both Omani and Britisher the victory of Nizwa was one to keep for telling to the grandchildren.

Sultan Said, after his exertions in the Jebel Akhdar War, retired to Salalah and here he was to stay for nearly ten years without once visiting his capital city, Muscat, or taking any active part in the governing of his country. Govern he certainly did, but it was in absentia and done through emissaries, by cables, by telephone. He had plans for Oman, but they were his own plans, to be carried out in his own time.

But Oman was not long to be left in peace for the spotlight now turns on Dhofar Province and in particular on South

Dhofar, some 700 miles to the south and separated from the rest of Oman by nothing but trackless desert and unfriendly coastline. It was here that an American oil company, peacefully and unsuccessfully prospecting, had one of its trucks blown up by a known trouble-maker named Ben Naful. A government guard was killed and Ben Naful fled across the border. When he returned it was undercover with arms, mines and equipment obtained from Saudi Arabia and Iraq and with the tacit support of Egypt. The 'Dhofar War' had begun.

5. The round tower of Nizwa fort showing the damage sustained during the Jebel Akhdar War, when the stronghold was captured by the forces of the Sultan of Oman

To understand the Dhofar War it is first necessary to get a working knowledge of the geography of the area. An area approximately the size of Wales, South Dhofar is largely mountainous but with a coastal plain some thirty miles wide at its widest on which is situated Salalah, the capital. North Dhofar, that is the part of the province north of the Qara Mountains, is all desert and practically uninhabited.

South Dhofar is 'round the corner' from the rest of Oman and because of this has a totally different climate, being subject to the monsoon which also affects the western shores of India. Both mountains and the coastal plain are fertile, vegetation is lush, producing vegetables and fruit unknown in the rest of Oman, while on the plain there are thousands of coconut palms. It has two distinct seasons and at times the vast rollers of the Arabian Sea provide a constant background roar as they crash on the miles of empty sandy beaches. It is a beautiful and wild coastline and as unlike the rest of Oman as the Channel coast from the Arabian Gulf. The monsoon which breaks in June and ends in October was to play a large part in the war, bringing as it does thick mists which roll down from Jebel, engulfing the plain and providing ideal cover for rebel troops. But this was to come later.

First let us go back to 1962 and to Sandhurst in England, where the young Qaboos bin Said, the only son of Sultan Said, was passing out as a second lieutenant in the Cameronians. Watching the new officers on their big day were members of their families and close friends as well as military dignitaries, but for the young man from Arabia there was no family present, only a middle-aged British major and his wife who had been detailed by his father to keep an eye on him and who were to exert such a tremendous influence on both father and son in the years to come. Major F. C. L. Chauncey, who had originally come to Muscat as British Consul in 1949, had retired in 1958 from the Foreign Service but, owing to his close friendship with Sultan Said, had returned almost immediately to Oman as the Sultan's personal adviser. Cast in the old colonial mould, for better and for worse, Major Chauncey, ex-Indian Army, took his job very seriously. He and Sultan Said were very much akin in character – autocratic, obstinate but with great integrity and even greater determination that Oman should progress only in their way and in their time.

With surprising forethought, Sultan Said decided to send his son round the world for three months to broaden his horizons. Accompanying the young man were the Chaunceys to guide the young Qaboos and to restrain any youthful enthusiasm which the Sultan himself so distrusted. But this broad-minded action towards his only son was to be the last.

It was in 1959 when Sultan Said retired permanently to his

palace in Salalah. Here with his handful of trusted advisers he worked out a careful programme of advancement for his country on a 'slowly, slowly' basis. To keep in this low gear he introduced ever more stringent rules and regulations, particularly regarding foreigners who came to work in the Sultanate. Local political prisoners were kept in confinement, often in chains, in the notorious fort of Jalali in Muscat and any tribal uprisings were dealt with ruthlessly. Sultan Said was taking no chances: his ancestors had almost without exception died at the hands of their near relatives and the Sultan had no wish to follow in their footsteps.

The young Qaboos personified to the Sultan the dangers of the future. At all costs he was not to be contaminated by the modern world. There was only one way to prevent this: to keep him isolated. Qaboos, who by this time was living near the Palace in Salalah, little realised that this would be his home for the next eight years.

In early 1964 an event occurred in Oman which was to interfere with all the Sultan's plans for the future, an event which, eventually, was to contribute more to his downfall than anything else. This was the decision of the oil company to go into commercial production. How many middle eastern countries had had their futures changed overnight by oil? The Sultan was determined this should not happen to Oman.

By 1968 revenue from oil had already reached £$25\frac{1}{2}$ million sterling in a year. The coffers were filling up down in Salalah, the gold ingots mounting in the bank, but the people of Oman still lived as they had always done and the young Qaboos was spending his formative years exiled among the elderly retainers, the books, the Koran and the slaves. And all the time more and more oil was coming to the surface, bringing with it the benefits but also the sludge and contamination of the modern world. And all the time the rebels in Dhofar were gaining ground.

By now the Palace cowered behind barbed wire and, as the monsoon mists crept along the plain, so the rebels came in closer and yet closer. It was not simply dissident tribesmen chafing against the yoke now, but a political movement fostered and encouraged by Communist Marxists from over the border in the People's Democratic Republic of Yemen. The problem could not be allowed to go on and the scales were slowly tipping. Outraged foreigners, Communist-inspired agents, Omanis forced

24 *Dawn Over Oman*

to live outside Oman due to impossible conditions at home, disgraced tribesmen all conspired to play the same game – the overthrowing of Sultan Said.

How many were finally involved in the palace coup of July 1970, will never be known but the only one to come out of the fracas with any real dignity would appear to have been the old Sultan himself, who personally fought a valiant battle up and down the dark and dusty corridors of the palace before being wounded, captured and bundled off in an RAF plane to Britain where he died in exile some two years later. The Sultan's Army, for whom no-one could feel anything but sorrow, were forced to play on both sides at once.

So the new era dawned. Qaboos, free at last, left Salalah and arrived in his capital city, Muscat, to a tumultuous and spontaneous welcome. None who were present will ever forget that memorable day – the quiet dignity of the young Sultan, the ten thousand gun-waving, drum-playing tribesmen at the airport of

6. The main street of Matrah, with the now-demolished Bab al Kabir or main gate, en fête for the arrival of Sultan Qaboos from Salalah in July 1970. After a competition later in the year, the plain red flag was replaced by a red, green and white one

Bait al Falaj, the miracle that no one was shot accidentally as museum piece guns stuttered into the air for the first time in centuries. The weeks that followed were intoxicating but no-one pretended the euphoria could last.

Back on the Omani scene from West Germany came Sayid Tariq bin Timur, uncle to the new Sultan. Tariq was installed as Prime Minister but soon changed his role to that of personal adviser and roving diplomat. Well-known Omani families who had been forced to live overseas during the stultifying rule of Sultan Said began to drift back to their own country. They brought not only a breath of fresh air from the outside world but an enthusiasm and expertise greatly needed in the awakening country. When Oman was accepted into the Arab League and later the United Nations in the year 1971, the peak of attainment was reached. Omanis held their heads high for the first time.

But the Dhofar War showed no signs of abating even though the root cause of the original rebellion had been removed. The

7. The Bab al Kabir in Muscat decorated for Sultan Qaboos' arrival, July 1970, when he entered his capital for the first time as ruler

Communists, in fact, were now stepping up their involvement and the Jebalis, the tough tribesmen from the mountains, were finding themselves increasingly recruited into a military force under all the rules of the Communist bosses. Across the border in Hauf, a revolutionary training camp was established in which young Jebalis were instructed in all military subjects before being sent back across the border to put their training into practice. The instructors carried little red books of Chairman Mao's thoughts – there was no doubt who was behind it all even without the added proof of captured Chinese weapons, a large hoard of which was captured in northern Oman in January 1973, just in time to prevent the movement spreading into the rest of the country.

Slowly the Sultan's Armed Forces began to get the upper hand but it was never easy. As Chairman Mao himself professed, 'a few men can keep a whole army on its toes indefinitely in the right sort of terrain'. And South Dhofar was very much the 'right sort of terrain'. It was a war that could have dragged on interminably but, fortunately for Oman, and thanks to increased aid from friendly powers (notably Iran and Jordan), the end did come at last and on 5 December 1975, the war was declared officially over. Since then there have inevitably been minor skirmishes and to date there are probably something like fifty guerillas still under arms left on Omani soil, but it is doubtful if even they regard themselves as being officially at war any longer. So the Dhofar War, always rather messy and inconclusive, came to a fitting end.

During its time, the war brought sorrow to the Jebalis but its most far-reaching effect has been that it took something like half of the national income over some six years which had to go on defence, an amount of money much resented by the Oman Government who had many better ways of spending it.

But there is another side to it. The wild countryside of South Dhofar has proved a perfect training ground for soldiers and, although until recently Oman was forced to rely on foreign officers to lead her army (mostly British seconded and contract officers), she now has a powerful nucleus of Omani officers, men of the new order whose first loyalty is to Sultan Qaboos. It could almost be said therefore that the Dhofar War was a blessing in disguise and in this case perhaps the Communists have not been so clever after all.

PART 2

3. The Background

Oman, although little known, is a comparatively large country, the distance from north to south approximating that between Beirut and Istanbul. With 1,700 kilometeres of shore line the entire land area is something like 300,000 square kilometres, 45,000 of which are mountainous. Of the remainder, 246,000 square kilometres is wadi and desert – at present infertile, barren and largely inhospitable. The coastal plain and inhabited area, a mere 9,000 square kilometres, is along the eastern and southern seaboard and largely cut off from outside by the desert, the 'interior'.

But it is the mountains that give Oman its character, it is the mountains that the traveller remembers and can never quite forget – the mountains that rise sheer for thousands upon thousands of feet, that are cut through by gorges no wider than a camel's breadth, mountains that in places drop sheer to the sea in a breathtaking abyss of weathered rock. Villages cling precariously to the sides of sheer rock faces in parts of the Jebel Akhdar: In Musandam villages perch atop the mountains like eagles' eyries while in South Dhofar, where the mountains drop

8. Typically dramatic mountain scenery in the Wadi Sahtan, showing geological strata upended

sheer into the Arabian Sea, little gems of beaches far below can be seen as though through the wrong end of a telescope. The incomparable mountains of Oman.

Almost as dramatic in a quieter, less aggressive but more ominous way is the desert. From the Umm as Samiim, the Salt Flats, in the west of Oman, the silent wastes of the Rub al Khali, the Empty Quarter, creep up upon one like the mists of time – nothing, nothing and yet more nothing as far as the eye can see. The silence is so deep here that ears ache from the very pressure of silence. One is alone with one's God now – this is what life is all about and there is nothing between Him and you. This is the type of country where Islam was born, in the silent wastes, where life is hard and often cruel but simple: simple enough for a man to find his God and where he can easily believe that God can find him.

But it has not always been so here. For millions of years Oman lay beneath the ocean until whole mountain ranges containing layer upon layer of rock that had been thrust upon each other over the centuries were thrown from the sea bed. Ophiolite was upended from as far down as the earth's very mantle to form the mountains we know today and to give them their name, the Jebel Akhdar, the Green Mountains. The upside-down geological features found in Oman are unique in this area and send geologists of today into ecstasies.

Far into the rocky wastes of the interior one can today pick up hundreds of fossilised shells. To stand on a red-hot, rocky wadi bed in the scorching sun and to let the tiny fossil shells run through one's fingers is to wonder anew. Nothing could seem further away than the sea, yet here in one's hands is the very proof that once the waves covered the rocks that are now too hot to touch, lying as they do in the choking desert dust.

Deeper still into the desert to the south near the border with the Yemen, where the rocky desert is brought up against the great sand dunes, geodes are found – round, knobbly and hollow, natural cannon balls lined with crystals of quartz and found only in a very few places in the world. Geologists find no trouble explaining what they are not, but what are they – well, that is something else and no explanation seems entirely satisfactory. What do they mean then, these geodes, how were they formed and what do they indicate? The answers must lie in the future.

But the fact that Oman was once under the sea raises questions with ready answers, answers that have already given her a new economy and put her on the map. For the inferences to be drawn from the geology and the fossil shells are a sure pointer to the presence of oil.

Oil originates from the decomposition of various animals and plants, mostly marine, that have been buried under layers of mud and silt sometimes for as long as 500 million years. The ideal locale is a large area of what are now or what have been shallow seas (e.g. in the Arabian Gulf). Ideally these decomposed marine forms are buried under layer upon layer of this mud and silt and the pressures therefrom, taken together with the temperature factor, combine to accelerate the process of oil and gas formation.

The oil thus formed can travel upwards from a depth of several thousand feet in any direction via cracks, malformations or just the natural porosity of rock, in small globules or in masses, often finding its own way to the surface. In the old days these oil seepages were regarded with awe and the oil was variously used in the preparation of medicine, in building and for heating. The fires often created from the gas seepages were called 'eternal fires' and were given mystical significance. In the mid-nineteenth century, in the first days of drilling for oil, rigs were erected near these seepages and it was not until some sixty years later that experts realised the importance of geology in locating underground oil reserves.

Rocks are divided into three main types – igneous rocks, sedimentary rocks and metamorphic rocks and it is with the second of these, the sedimentary, that oil geologists are mainly concerned. Sedimentary basins are always worth investigating for the presence of oil and many occur among the margins and foothills bordering mountain chains. By far the most productive of these world sedimentary basins lies in the Middle East. Shallow seas of warm water favour growth of corals and algae which contribute to the formation of carbonate rocks such as limestone (formed of plant and animal life – corals, worms, crinoids, molluscs etc.) and dolomite (consisting mainly of magnesium carbonate and calcium carbonate). By the study of fossils the geologist can date the deposits of sediment and separate the layers of beds. Generally speaking the younger rocks tend to

9. Travellers in the Wadi Sarami take a break after crossing a water splash

provide more oil, the older rocks having lost much in the process of seepages over the centuries.

If this were all, oil exploration would be comparatively simple but such is not the case. During the earth's history, the crust of the earth's surface has been in continual movement – underground upheavals, weathering, erosion, always the surface is changing – the layers change places, are tipped sideways, are lifted up, buried, great folds occur. Some of these folds of stratified rock have strata sloping downwards in the opposite direction. These are called anticlines, the opposite to synclines, and can vary in width from a few hundred metres up to many kilometres. Sometimes these folds are stressed beyond their points of resistance and then 'faults' occur which can displace the beds on either side thousands of metres. There is nothing predictable about the earth's surface.

Oil exploration today consists of the provision of a detailed geological survey of the area, of an evaluation of the possibilities based on this knowledge and of an interpretation of all the data received from seismic parties. These parties, working on the 'echo sounding' principle may, with the use of a 'thumper' or by the laying of dynamite, produce maps of the underground strata from which the evaluation can be made. Today, more and more, computers are being used to evaluate all the data thus obtained. Aerial survey can also play a large part in the exploration of new territory.

When the area appears promising, exploration wells, 'wildcats', are drilled. A successful wildcat is a 'discovery well', an unsuccessful one a 'dry hole'. The early history of exploration in Oman consisted largely of dry holes.

Oil exploration in Oman goes back as far as 1925 when the d'Arcy Exploration Company (first formed by William Knox d'Arcy as a subsidiary of Anglo-Persian when he struck a gusher in Persia) obtained a two-year exploration licence from Sultan Taimur bin Feisal, grandfather of the present ruler. Landing from the sea, a geological party carried out a number of traverses inland from the Batinah coast but the d'Arcy licence was allowed to lapse after its initial unproductive two years. In 1937 the IPC Group obtained a concession for seventy-five years, the company being known first as Petroleum Concessions Ltd (Shareholders being Shell, BP, CFP and Near East Development Corporation each with 23¾ per cent and Partex with 5 per cent) and later as Petroleum Development (Oman & Dhofar) Ltd. It was, however, an unfortunate time to choose – time only for one brief and inconclusive geological exploration in 1938–9 before the onset of the Second World War. In 1951 the Company's name changed to Petroleum Development (Oman) Ltd, Dhofar having been relinquished earlier.

The next milestone on the oil road in Oman came with the American scientist and adventurer, Dr Wendell Phillips. In 1950 Dr Phillips was invited by the Imam of Yemen to excavate the Moon temple at Mareb, the ancient capital of the Queen of Sheba. Phillips and his party were attacked by Yemeni bandits, fled across the desert leaving most of their equipment behind and were befriended by Said bin Timur, the Sultan of Muscat and Oman. The bandit attack proved a blessing in disguise, for Said bin Timur took an instant liking to this twentieth-century buccaneer and made him his economic adviser. In an almost embarrassing moment of goodwill he also presented Dr Phillips with the oil concession for Dhofar which, at the time, must have rendered the verbose Californian speechless for perhaps the first time in his life.

Wendell Phillips, who confessed to knowing next to nothing about oil concessions, rushed to New York to arrange the financing of exploration and thereby embarked on a career that was to turn him into one of the world's leading oil personalities and a self-made millionaire twice over. But not from Dhofar oil – the concession, assigned to a subsidiary of Cities Service & Richfield with Phillips taking a 2½ per cent share was not to prove any more successful than it had for IPC. By 1961 Cities Service & Richfield had a thousand men in the field and had spent between thirty and forty million dollars. They had drilled twenty-three wells – all dry, or nearly dry holes. The last gamble on Dhofar was taken by Mecom but this, too, proved unsuccessful.

There was no doubt that oil existed in Dhofar but so far it had been the very heavy crude, sluggish to move and infinitely difficult to transport in a province whose shores are subjected to the monsoon and the high seas it brings. Anyway, by this time the spotlight had turned on Central Oman.

In 1954 Petroleum Development (Oman) Ltd, as it was known, had landed in the Duqm area, just south of Masirah

Island, working inland from there and during October of the same year the first survey was carried out by geologists on the Fahud structure, previously noted by aerial reconnaissance. At the end of 1955, the company decided on Azaiba, some thirty miles north of Muscat, as the base camp area, with Saih al Maleh as a marine base and with a road through the Sumail Gap as the main link with Fahud and the interior. In January 1956 the first well was 'spudded in' at Fahud.

Between 1956 and 1960 four exploration wells were drilled – at Fahud, Ghaba, Heima and Afar. In addition two seismic parties and a gravity party operated throughout most of the period. By the end of March 1960 some £12 million had been expended by the IPC Group in Oman with little result. How near they had been, though, was to be discovered four years later when oil was struck at Fahud the second time around – and only some 400 yards from the first unsuccessful drilling!

On 24 October 1960, however, with no oil in sight, British Petroleum, CFP and Near East Development Corporation withdrew from the IPC group. The shareholding then became Shell 85 per cent and Partex 15 per cent, CFP rejoining the venture later, on 8 June 1967, by purchasing 10 per cent of the Partex-held 15 per cent. This percentage stood until the end of 1973.

By 1964 the Company decided they had discovered oil in sufficient quantities to warrant production and in March of that year they announced plans to that effect following discoveries at Yibal (1962), Natih (1963) and Fahud (1964). Three years later a new and revised agreement was signed, covering the unexpired period of the 1937 concessions, the terms similar to those in force in other oil-producing countries in the area.

In August 1967, commercial oil was exported from Oman for the first time. If there was a watershed in Oman's history this was it, the point of no return, the point from which the Sultanate was set on the road to prosperity even if it was not to be evident for some years yet to come. By 1967 PD Oman Ltd had spent more than £25 million sterling in providing export facilities for oil at Saih al Maleh, a main-line pumping station at Fahud and a housing area at Ras al Hamra plus many fringe facilities – communications, transport, a hospital. The oil age in Oman had begun, but it was not to be all plain sailing by any means. The production target of 360,000 barrels per day set for the first quarter of 1970 had to be reduced to 320,000 barrels in the second quarter and 310,000 barrels in the third quarter. Exploration proved disappointing – and then disaster struck.

On 16 August 1970, only one month after Sultan Qaboos came to power, oil men were going about their jobs in Yibal field, some 650 kilometres into the interior of Oman near the Umm as Samiim and bordering the Empty Quarter. Yibal was then producing oil at the rate of 300,000 barrels a day, oil which would be pumped across the desert and mountains to the waiting tankers at Mina al Fahal on the coast. There were two crews in the area working on two drilling rigs. On rig 4, over well 14, drillers were working their way down through the Wasia, the gas-bearing strata now called the Natih. Below that lay the oil – it was a routine drilling. Night fell and at the camp, some two miles away, the evening shift had just returned to their caravans, had their showers and retired to their bunks when there was an almighty roar, one of the most terrifying sounds in the modern world – the noise of a 'blow-out'.

A 'blow-out' is the uncontrolled release of high-pressure gas and, not only is it dangerous because of the fire risk involved, but the cost of regaining control can be phenomenal, added to which, of course, the actual loss of oil and gas must be taken into account.

Loss of life was minimal, only one driller dying of burns in spite of the efforts of his friends to pull him away from the blazing inferno that had been rig 4. It was a miracle the loss of life was not higher.

The Red Adair Company from Texas, the world's number one oil fire fighters, were called in, but it was not until five months later that the blow-out was finally brought under control – at an estimated cost of some £2½ million sterling. Yibal 14 was a name to be reckoned with.

Today, it is difficult to find the exact location of the blow-out. The dozens of caravans that housed the men engaged in fighting it have vanished, so has all the equipment, the mud lake and the acres of mud created when Yibal 14 started to spew out water before it finally died. Yibal now boasts a water injection plant and only a skeleton staff checks dials and sees all is in order. The flares are now organised flares, the regular burning off of surplus gas – routine flickers of fire across the miles of sandy wastes.

In 1972 PDO discovered more oil at Ghaba North, Qarn Alam, Saih Nihayda and Habur, followed in 1973 by a further discovery at Saih Rawl, the most promising of all. By this time two questions were uppermost in the minds of the oilmen and the Oman Government – whether oil could be found in marketable quantities in Dhofar and whether it would be worthwhile to develop natural gas.

Extensive drilling programmes in Dhofar during 1974–5 resulted in a clearer definition of accumulations at Amal and Marmul and, by the end of 1977, oil had been discovered at Rahab. This oil, however, was of a poor quality, thick and difficult to transport. The problems of getting the oil to the coast north over the desert or south to an unfriendly coast subject to monsoons were almost insurmountable. However, a new discovery in the spring of 1978 at Qaharir, south of Marmul, produced oil of a better quality altogether, enabling the pipeline to be linked, via the Amal fields, to join the main line at Fahud. By 1980, when these fields come on stream, they should at least counterbalance the expected drop in existing fields, keeping production steady at around 300,000 barrels a day.

The Government of Oman always showed great interest in the exploitation of natural gas. In consequence a gas-line project, built by an Italian company with PD Oman Ltd, and Shell International Petroleum Maatschapij as consultants to supervise the execution, was instigated. This involved the laying of a line some 320 kilometres from Yibal field to Ghubrah on the Batinah coast, a project which was completed in 1978. This natural gas will provide energy for the electricity generating and the desalination plants at Ghubrah, and later also for a large cement works to be built nearby and for numerous other industrial projects.

From all this it will be obvious that PDO has played a large and very vital part in the shaping of Oman today. There have been other oil companies in the past and there will be more in the future but PDO's contribution has been incalculable, not only for the revenue earned but for the training she has given to Omanis both in their own country and overseas and in the establishment of trade schools, hospitals and clinics. The relationship between the oil company and the country itself is unique.

Although not officially a member of OPEC or OAPEC, Oman obtained full participation terms as from 1 January 1974.

Other than oil there has been much speculation in Oman regarding the possible mineral deposits. Copper had always been a distinct possibility, and in February 1974 the Government announced that copper deposits had been found in the Sultanate by a Canadian-based mineral development group (Marshall

10. Sultan Qaboos signing the first Participation Agreement with officials of Petroleum Development (Oman) Ltd

Oman Exploration Inc. and Prospection Ltd), in sufficient quantities to warrant further development. The Government further added they they were financing the project to the tune of 51 per cent to stimulate further exploration of minerals. This is the first time that Government participation in a mineral agreement has been obtained in the Gulf area and is an indication of how determined Oman is to find sources of revenue other than oil.

Apart from copper, asbestos has been found in encouraging quantities and coal and manganese are also possibilities. Traces of other minerals have been found but not in appreciable quantities and not worth commercial exploitation. On the whole, however, mineral exploration has been encouraging and it is just possible that minerals could be the main source of revenue when oil supplies dwindle to insignificant quantities (at the present time and in the absence of future discoveries, this is put at anything between fifteen and twenty years from now).

No country wishes to have such a one-sided economy based entirely on oil, Oman, with her limited natural resources, least of all. But it is a fairly common problem in the world today and Oman is not alone in facing it. And – like the others – she owes much to her desert.

4. *The Desert*

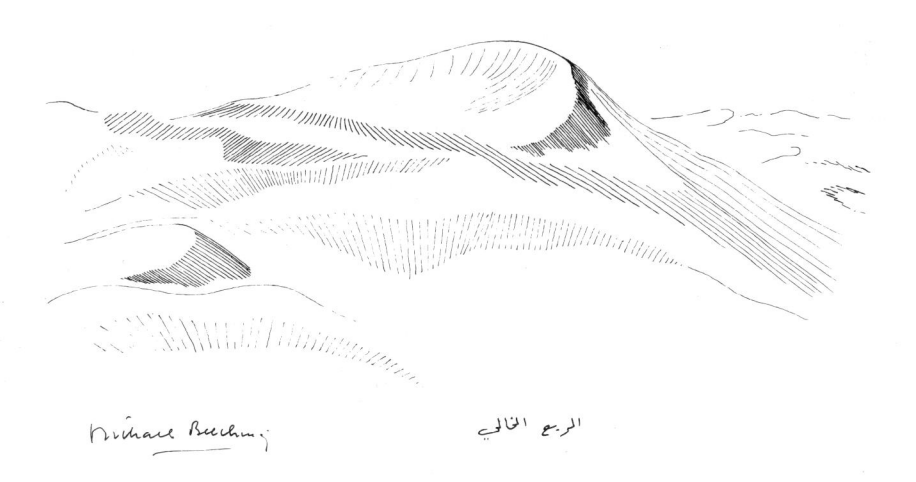

Oman as we have seen is largely desert, but the term 'desert' covers a wide range of country. Most of Oman's desert is, in fact, rocky waste, scarred by wadi beds and nowadays by tracks left by Land Rovers and trucks. But there is also desert in the accepted sense of the word – rolling sand dunes, soft sand dunes and oases, startling in their greenery and blissful in their sound of running water.

The deserts of Oman are peopled by the Badawi or Bedouin, 'Bedu' as they are commonly called. There are something like fifty different tribes (many of these subdivided) in Oman today but the Bedu are mainly from the Bait Kathir, the Duru, the Janabah and the Harasis. The Duru have become particularly rich and well-known since the discovery of oil as most of the fields have been found in Duru country and in consequence most of the labour has of necessity been recruited from this tribe.

The Bedu are nomadic, semi-nomadic or sedentary. They are something of a law unto themselves – fiercely loyal to their own tribe, hospitable in the extreme to the passing traveller and with ideas of their own as regards raiding and the purloining of others' property. The average Bedu is larger than life, rugged, humorous and intensely religious. Allah is with him always and his conversation is always interspersed with 'By Allah', 'Thanks be to God', 'God willing', 'Go with God' and so on.

Here was where Islam began and has been nurtured in its pure form over the centuries. Here are no great mosques, no muezzin to call the faithful to prayer but

> 'The true mosque in a pure and holy heart
> Is builded: there let all men worship God
> For there He dwells, not in a mosque of stone.'

It is not surprising that the adult Bedu is tough, for the life is hard and it is very much a case of the survival of the fittest. The Bedu baby is born to a hard world, bathed first in camel's urine, swaddled in a plaster of camel dung and later left to fend for himself in an unfriendly world of flies, scorpions, fleas and diseases which he must endure cheerfully. And cheerfully he

11. Prevailing winds turn the Wahhiba sand-dunes into a rippling sea of gold as the sun rises

does endure, for the little Bedu is by and large the most happy and entertaining of fellows though his nose is invariably running and his eyes are covered in flies. But his smile is contagious and irresistible. Even Bedu women tend to keep more cheerful than their town sisters though their lot is a hard one. There is a sisterhood of the desert as well as a brotherhood, brought about no doubt by the necessity of sticking together to combat the vagaries of their wayward menfolk, and also by the scarcity of baubles which distract their sex the world over.

Next in importance – often it must be said in fairness even before the womenfolk – comes the camel. The Arabic word for camel approximates the word for 'beautiful' and to a Bedu a camel is not only beautiful but an all-provider – a means of transport and a beast of burden whose milk is a delicacy, whose urine a disinfectant and purge, whose dung a fuel, whose flesh sweet and whose hide strong. A man is measured in stature by the number of camels he owns. They are his capital and his insurance for the future and the number of camels he must part with to purloin a wife or marry off a daughter causes him much heart-searching.

Omani camels are particularly famous for both their speed and their stamina. As one Arab proverb says, 'Do not ride an Oman she-camel and do not marry a girl from the Za'ab tribe. The former will upset the pace of the army, the latter will upset your wives.' The best racing camels in Oman come from the Batinah coast and also from the Sharqiya, south of Muscat in the area of the Wahhiba sands. The Duru also boast a famous breed of camel which are alleged to be even hardier than the Batinah ones. This is probably due to geography as the Duru country borders the Empty Quarter and the camels there are conditioned to survival in the vast desert wastes.

A mystery of the desert to the casual traveller is what the camels live on at all. A camel is usually to be seen chomping away with apparent relish at the camel-thorn bush, a prickly scrub with long, razor-sharp thorns. May Allah preserve their leather-lined stomachs! A camel can in fact live on the minimum of water, going for as long as a week without any at all and for ten days without food. During these waterless days camels survive on water drawn from their tissues and on water created as a breakdown product of fat. The hump is filled largely with fat accumulated at times when food and water are plentiful and the weight of the hump can be up to thirty pounds. After a period of abstention from drinking a camel can take in as much as twenty-five gallons of water at one time. A student of the Arabic language is usually told that any Arabic word the meaning of which he looks up can mean either what it says, the exact opposite or something to do with a camel. It is safe to say that there are at least thirty words for a camel in Arabic, describing not only the sex but the age, whether or not the she-camel is pregnant, if so for how long (the period of gestation for a camel is one year), and other fascinating details.

The Bedu is an almost uncanny tracker and can often tell by looking at the footprints of a camel the whole history of the beast – where it is from, where it is going, whether it is a male or female, if the latter whether it is pregnant, if it had a rider – the information seems endless.

12. A proud camel-owner poses for a picture before setting out on his lonely journey which may take many days

Bedu hospitality is traditional all over the Arab world but in Oman it is not simply a code of honour or a book of rules but a hospitality that comes from the heart. Here there are no solemn greetings with stylised questions and answers but a boisterous welcome for a traveller that remains in his memory wherever he travels in the future.

I once spent a few days visiting various Duru tribes in the area of the Wadi Aswad, west of Nizwa. Late one afternoon we ground over the sand dunes in our two Land Rovers, apparently in the middle of nowhere, to keep a rendezvous with the local tribe. Over the top of a particularly large dune we were confronted by an incredible sight. The sun was just setting behind a large samarra tree in which hung several goatskins of water silhouetted black against the red sky, a sky that turned the rippling sand dunes into golden waves. Among the dunes some twenty tribesmen, their silver khanjars glittering in the fast fading sunlight, had assembled, spreading exotic, brilliantly patterned carpets over the sand.

As the Land Rovers ground down the sand dune and stopped, they all got up and rushed towards us, waving their rifles and greeting us with hugs and warm double handshakes and we were at once enveloped by large laughing Bedu, their bandoliers of cartridges, their daggers and their rifles. They motioned us to sit down on the carpets and soon we were sipping steaming coffee and eating some of the best halwa we had ever tasted. There was no objection to our photographing them – that indeed was the purpose of our visit – and the faces around us were some of the strongest and finest we had seen anywhere. It was one of those experiences that are larger than life the memory of which lasts a lifetime.

Bedu hospitality, of course, works both ways, as indeed it should. 'If you show a Badawi the entrance of your house, then open wide the door that his camel also may enter', states the proverb. One can sense here the deep rift between the town dweller and the desert dweller and the patronising tone of the former for the latter. But in the desert the Bedu comes into his own, where his knowledge of the scanty water wells, the correct reading of a footprint in the sand, his uncanny sense of direction can mean all the difference between life and death. Here your town dweller is as a newborn baby. Many do drive the deserts these days in their Land Rovers but few realise the dangers. A sudden wind blows, the ground begins to heave and shimmer. In a flash tyre tracks, footprints, all traces of man and beast are obliterated and a pleasant weekend's outing could easily become a nightmare tragedy. It never does to underestimate the desert.

Yet when one is really lost in the desert and one can see that this could easily be the end, it is not fear that is the predominant emotion – more a kind of awe and a realisation of the immensity of nature as opposed to the fragility of man. Perhaps we should all experience this feeling sometime in our lives to cut us down to size.

It is here in this wilderness that the Bedu has learned to live his life, and he has scant regard for the so-called joys of civilisation. His predominant loyalty is to the tribe, for a man without a tribe is nothing, and honour is all important. He accepts all trials and

13. An early-morning meeting in the desert between a donkey-rider and a Bedu with his camel. Omanis ride their donkeys sitting on its hindquarters, a strange sight to foreigners

tribulations as the will of Allah and regards himself and his fellow Bedu as Allah's chosen people. It is no wonder that the Bedu is so enraptured with his God, for every day he is surrounded by the vastness of the desert wastes and every night he sees the same vastness in the night sky above him. What else can he feel but his own insignificance, what else can he say but 'God is Great'.

The Bedu is fanatically loyal to his friends but pitiless to his enemies, though the law of sanctuary is sacred. Famous is the story of the two young men who fought each other. One was killed and the other escaped and fled, finally seeking sanctuary in the nearest tent when the avengers began to catch up with him. The tent in which he sought sanctuary turned out to belong to the murdered man's father yet still this sanctuary was respected and the murderer became as another son in the household.

The Bedu has a picturesque form of speech and will never use one word when five will do. His turn of invective is delightful to western ears and his similes and metaphors unusual in the extreme. 'Oh, you piece of dirt in the navel' is a favourite term of abuse, and many similar ones relate to the more unpleasant functions of a camel. My own favourite is 'Of the hundred pairs of shoes outside your mother's bedroom, which pair belonged to your father?' So much more descriptive than its western one-word equivalent.

The desert-dweller is a great story-teller. Stories of past exploits, of half-forgotten legends and witchcraft are kept for the long evenings, to be told around the camp fire when one's listeners are tired from the day's march and when darkness outside the firelight lends itself to tales of murder and mystery. It is almost impossible to pin a Bedu down when trying to understand a story or extract information and there can be many explanations in answer to a question, any one or all possibly true. As an example – all over the desert in Oman one finds scrub bushes to which have been tied pieces of rag. One explanation is that mothers with ailing children tie pieces of the child's clothes to the trees to get the strength of the trees transferred to the child. Yet these rags are often used as signposts and a Bedu will often say to a traveller, 'Go two hours' (this would probably mean by camel and indicate about eight miles) 'then turn where the blue rag is tied to the bush'. It seems a more likely explanation certainly.

The open spaces of the desert can prove very monotonous indeed to the casual traveller but it need not be so, for even the deserts in Oman are full of surprises. For example, one hundred and fifty kilometres south of the Jebel Salakh in Central Oman, in an area where in all directions nothing more than a scrub bush or an occasional pile of rocks breaks the monotony for hour upon empty hour, six rocky mounds can be seen rising to heights of over 150 metres, all within an area of some 1,000 square kilometres. These mounds are called 'salt piercements' by the geologists and occur where layers of salt whose specific gravity is less than the surrounding rocks have been pushed to the surface and beyond by the pressure of harder, denser rocks such as dolomite. This harder rock forms a cap over the salt piercement which is sometimes pushed aside, showing the salt underneath. Under these mounds, where centuries of dripping water have dissolved the salt, caves have formed and, where the salt still drips, stalactites and stalagmites have grown, sparkling with salt crystals and reflecting the light in a million tiny facets. To explore the caves in summer, when the outside sun temperature may be as high as 80° C or more is to find a sudden fairyland in the middle of hell, a cool, dark cavern where the wandering torchlight or the stray shaft of sunlight reflects on the crystallised formations in thousands of tiny pinpoints of light.

One of the six caves in this particular area is Qara Qarat Kibrit (Kibrit in Arabic meaning sulphur or matches). The amount of sulphur there today is negligible but patches can still be seen outside the main cave together with so-called 'red salt', salt that has been exposed to the sun, melted and reformed after absorbing impurities such as iron. In the past the Bedu used the sulphur to treat the camels for Garab, a skin disease like mange. The sulphur was mixed with charcoal (obtained by burning wood) and mixed with water to a paste which was put on the affected area. Now, of course, the treatment is more modern and very much simpler. But the salt is still used by the wandering Bedu for cooking purposes. Although that at Kibrit is not of the best quality it is easily obtained as the stalactites and stalagmites are brittle and break off easily. Nearby at Qarat al Milh, the salt is of better quality but is harder to get at and must be dug from the ground.

Normally caves like these could have remained practically undisturbed for centuries except for the occasional Bedu but, with the discovery of oil in the area, the desert is fast becoming criss-crossed with tracks which are traversed regularly now by oilmen and contractors. More people than ever before are travelling the desert regularly, and those who are interested enough to look beyond the normal discomforts find a new world opening up.

Something else to break the monotony of desert travel is the 'sand-devil' which one can see almost any time and anywhere in the deserts of Oman. A sudden small whirlwind will whip up the sand into a whirling dervish who flies away at a great rate, dust and pebbles swept up into the vortex. Driving along the tracks one is often met by a sand-devil and, for a split second, all is turmoil until the devil rushes away always in a tearing hurry. The local people call them spirits of the dead – who knows?

But the most intriguing phenomena in the Oman desert, as in the great deserts anywhere, is the mirage, seen usually in summer when temperatures soar above 50°C and most Bedu sleep away the day and travel, if they must, by night. Suddenly on the horizon beautiful stretches of calm water appear, reflecting trees and scrub. For a time the apparition is suspended, as it were, above the line of the horizon but as the traveller approaches it disappears. However much one knows that what one sees is only a mirage there is always the faint hope that – well, this time it could be just what it seems and in an hour or so one could be on the edge of that placid lake, drinking, throwing water over one's sand-encrusted skin and bathing one's blistered feet. At times like these one could sell one's soul for the very feel of cool, sweet water.

But it is not to be so, for the mirage retreats as one gets nearer and one settles back into a sunbaked stupor to await some landmark, a landmark which, even when seen, may take some hours to catch up with. At night when one is approaching the oilfields one can often see the red glow of the gas flares in the far distance but it does not do to start thinking of the end of the trail, of water or of food, for it can still mean a three or four hour journey.

And how strange it is these days in Oman, after hour upon hour of sweat-stained, exhausting desert travel, to come suddenly upon a group of tents or caravans and, like a mirage come true, there is air-conditioning, water unlimited, ice-cold drinks and, of course food. Sometimes it seems little short of a miracle.

The oilmen and contractors in Oman today are helping to transform the desert by teaching the Bedu they employ how to make life that much pleasanter in impossible surroundings. Sanitation is an example. The nomad is also tasting the joys of civilisation – a varied diet, constant sweet water, even radio and the cinema. He will never be quite the same again.

He is also learning a strange and peculiar jargon with which he is spattering his everyday conversation. Sitting with a group of Bedu one night round the fire, a recent traveller who was spending a few days with the Harasis put up a hand to signify he had eaten enough. The Sheikh, who spoke nothing other than tribal dialect, shook his head. 'Full tank?' he enquired solicitously.

Oil is indeed changing the deserts of Oman if not quite to the same extent as the coastal area. But to the west of the furthest drilling rig or seismic camp, across the acres of salt flats called the Umm as Samiim, the Mother of Salt, the Empty Quarter beckons the traveller, tongue in cheek. Man has a long way to go yet in taming the desert.

5. *The Cities*

A Persian poet once described Muscat by saying it 'gives to the panting sinner a living anticipation of his future destiny'. This, of course, refers to the temperature, which in summer can reach fearful proportions, coupled with the fact that both Muscat and Matrah are surrounded by mountains which retain the heat and successfully prevent any wind from alleviating the sufferings of the population. Today many of the more fortunate inhabitants of both towns boast air-conditioners, but there are still many others who spend the summer nights lying on the roof tossing and sweating in vain efforts to sleep without suffocating. And yet another misery has been added only recently – an almost constant cacophony of hooting and brake screeching which goes on well into the early hours.

But in spite of their sufferings inhabitants of Muscat would seldom change their abode and foreigners particularly are stout defenders of the town as a place to live. All visitors without exception are enchanted by their first glimpse of it, either from the sea or, more usually, from the top of the hill as they drive down into the bowl and catch their first view of the harbour, looking much as it has done for centuries.

Few harbours in the world can be as picturesque as Muscat. Of classic crescent shape, it is dominated by the twin forts of Mirani and Jalali named, it is said, after a Portuguese commander 'Mur' and a Persian commander 'Jalal', though there are differing explanations and it is also claimed that Mirani, once known as Fort Capitan under the Portuguese, may have got its name from 'Admirale', successor to Capitan.

Fort Mirani is built into the side of the mountain on the western side of the harbour and is one of the finest forts in Oman. It was built late in the sixteenth century by the Portuguese, the date of completion being given in an inscription over the inner gateway:

> 'In the reign of the very high and mighty Philip first of this name, our sacred king, in the eighth year of his reign in the crown of Portugal, he ordered through Dom Duarte de Menezes his viceroy in India that this fortress should be

14. Muscat harbour today. Upper left is Fort Mirani with Sultan Qaboos' palace to its right. The fortifications in the foreground are part of the old city walls

built which Belchior Alvares built, the first captain and founder. 1588.'*

Outside the fort was an area for the execution of prisoners sentenced to death which was in use until a few years ago while nearby, in an open space near the old Khor jetty, was the site of the slave-market. A road now runs west along the coast from Khor jetty to the new Naval Base at Mukallah which has been built on the side of the old coaling station. Today smart new patrol boats of the Sultan's Navy take the place of the one dhow, until 1970 Oman's sole naval vessel.

*It was not the first fort on the site – a previous one still under construction was destroyed by Turkish cannonfire during the siege of Muscat by the Turkish fleet of Piri Pacha in 1552.

15. Muscat harbour: the continuation of photograph 14. Upper right is Fort Jalali

By 1588 the Portuguese grip on the area was already weakening and they decided to turn Muscat into a Portuguese stronghold by taking advantage of the natural defences and building the two forts which have changed little in appearance in the last 350 years. In 1610 a sea-level bastion incorporating a gun platform was added to the fortifications in an endeavour to prevent small boats running into Muscat cove out of range of the large cannon. An inscription reads: 'Experience, zeal and truth built for me the defense of the cross which defends me, in the order of the very high and powerful king Don Philip, third of this name, in the year 1610.' But by this time the days of the Portuguese were indeed numbered and in 1649 the troops of the Imam Sultan bin Saif entered the town. Most of the Portuguese, some 600 of them, were evacuated by sea but many others fled into Fort Mirani. Food supplies were inadequate, however, and the garrison was forced to surrender.

Except for a brief period in 1743–4, when it was occupied by the Persians, Fort Mirani has been in Omani hands ever since. The cannon atop the fort are used today exclusively for welcoming ships from foreign navies on courtesy calls and many a hardened sailor must have felt a lump in his throat at the sheer romance of entering the old rock-girt harbour to the roar of cannonfire. It always seems to the observer that so many things can go wrong it would take a miracle to fire the cannon at the right time and place, but somehow the miracle always happens and they have not sunk a ship yet, though there was an occasion when both fort and ship wore their respective flags upside down – no doubt the commander on the fort was having his problems with the cannon while the ship's commander was probably too overwhelmed to concentrate.

Jalali, known to the Portuguese as San Joao, dates from 1589 and is a gloomy forbidding prison straddling the high cliffs on the eastern side of the harbour where occupants were until recently kept chained to the walls, often for no greater crime than political disagreement with the existing regime. It is almost impossible for us to comprehend the miseries suffered by erstwhile prisoners in Jalali and I am always reminded of a poem I came across in an unpretentious little book called *The Life of Umar the Great, Second Caliph of Islam* by one Shibli Numani:

> Alack, Alack, my sorrow's cup
> Is full to brim. My comrades free
> Are tilling out on yonder field
> All shackled while I lie. Ah me
> These ponderous fetters weigh me down,
> My efforts are of no avail
> The doors are shut, in vain I cry
> Oh, shall I never leave this Jail?

It is hardly surprising that one of the first acts of Sultan Qaboos bin Said when he came to power in 1970 was to free all but a few prisoners from the fort, a symbolic action much appreciated by the people of Oman. The prisoners themselves must have been completely overwhelmed and for days they wandered around still toting bits of chain and leg irons attached to their ankles and with a glazed look on their faces.

In 1963 occurred the only mass escape from Jalali when over forty prisoners managed to get away. Their freedom did not last long, however, and all but one were captured within a stone's throw.

Seen towards evening from the eastern side, silhouetted black against the red of the setting sun, Jalali is as forbidding a sight as one could imagine and one prisoner who escaped alone from the fort took one look at his surroundings and went straight back.

Along the steep sides of the cliffs are many flat rock surfaces and on these generations of sailors have written the names of their ships. Sultan Said bin Timur used to call Muscat his 'Marine Autograph Book' and many famous ship names appear as well as those of small craft and even individuals trying to claim immortality the easy way.

At the foot of Jalali itself, on a neighbouring rock face, is a white ensign said to have been painted originally by Nelson himself, when a midshipman in the *Perseus* whose name appears above it. True or not, it is a likely story for Muscat's famous 'visitors' book' is a history book in itself and Nelson's White Ensign is in fact marked on Admiralty charts, Muscat being known to many young naval personnel for this reason alone.

One prominent name is the *Eskimo*, the first Tribal class frigate to visit Muscat, which arrived in 1960 on the same day as Lord

56 *Dawn Over Oman*

Carrington, then Minister of State. To mark the occasion, which was a first-time visit for both ship and peer, Sultan Said bin Timur sent down gifts to them both. The ship got a handsome silver coffee pot and Lord Carrington a very heavy suitcase which, on opening, was found to contain a hundredweight of halwa, the sticky sweet favoured all over the Arab world. Obvi-

16. Part of Sultan Said bin Timur's marine 'autograph book', where generations of seamen have carved the names and ports of registry of their ships. The original of HMS *Perseus* (centre) was said to have been carved by Nelson

ously the presents had got mixed up somewhere along the line and one wonders if Lord Carrington took all the halwa back home to England or whether he and the captain of the frigate did a quiet exchange when no-one was looking.

The majority of ships whose names appear in the 'visitors' book' are naval vessels, but among the minority are several small cargo ships like the *Leninogorsk*, around 9,000 tons. It is amusing to think of the serious-faced Russian seamen with their buckets of whitewash climbing stoically up the cliffs to appease what must, to most of them, have seemed a very frivolous and decadent tradition.

Many of the ship's visits can only be traced now through the records of cemeteries in which many of the sailors found their last resting places. A surprising number of sailors did end their days in Muscat and one ship, the *Khuzistan*, even left her captain in a Muscat grave. The graves themselves are in two quiet coves, the Sheikh Jabber cove and the Sa'ali cove, east of the main harbour and reached only by sea through a narrow channel that runs below Jalali. Many of the headstones are awry today and many inscriptions illegible, but it is hardly surprising for the next-of-kin of those buried below are themselves dead now and resting in other graves half a world away in places like Devon or Kent. But distance is no longer important to them and the gulls wheel overhead as they do there.

One could be forgiven for thinking that World War II passed Muscat by, but such was not the case for a Japanese submarine daringly shot a torpedo through the same narrow channel leading back into the harbour and blew up a merchantman anchored there. The sheer audacity of the Japanese commander deserves to go down in history.

Also at the foot of Jalali is the British Embassy, for a long time the British Consulate-General. A beautiful old building with thick heavy walls capable of withstanding a siege and floors that rock in rather an alarming manner, it must be one of the most picturesque embassies in the world. Until recently in the large courtyard outside, which commands a magnificent panoramic view of the harbour, stood the famous flagpole. Any slave who could make his way into the compound and embrace the pole was given his freedom and a certificate of 'manumission' to prove it. Copies of this certificate are still lodged at the Embassy though it is some fifteen years since anyone took advantage of the offer as Sultan Said decreed that any slave wishing to be free had only to approach his local Wali for the necessary document. It is only fair to say that very few did as slaves of the royal household had always been very well treated.

| الدولة البهية القيصرية الأنكليس | | BRITISH GOVERNMENT |
| ورقـــة العتق | | MANUMISSION CERTIFICATE |

Be it known to all who may see this that the bearer _____ aged about _____ years has been manumitted and no one has a right to interfere with his/her liberty. Dated _____ this _____ day of _____ 19 ___

Signature & Designation of British Representative

17. Certificate of manumission. Slaves who took sanctuary by embracing the flagpole in the British Consulate-General were 'manumitted', or set free

A new palace which now adorns the Muscat waterfront is already beginning to merge into the scenery and in a few years time will not too seriously impair the age-old view of the town.

The preservation of Muscat has been a constant care of the Government who have engaged special architects to see that the town is saved from indiscriminate development. Of the three largest and most famous houses – Bait Graiza, Bait Nadir and Bait Ghaliya – only Bait Graiza has been added to and improved to any great extent in its new role as a rest-house for visiting dignitaries. Of the remainder, Bait Nadir is now the home of the National Museum and Bait Ghaliya, the one-time French consulate building, is still privately occupied. There are, of course, quite a number of new buildings, some of which could quite happily be spirited away, and many old ones which have been renovated or strengthened, but basically Muscat has not changed too much and one can still recapture its enchantment without too much difficulty.

New finds are constantly coming to light in Muscat today and one of the most interesting was a stone column base and two column drums from the Portuguese convent of the Augustinian friars discovered close to the foot of Fort Mirani. The convent was built shortly after the two main forts and was described by Don Garcia da Silva, the Spanish Ambassador to the Shah of Persia, who stayed there soon after its completion in 1617. It had accommodation for fifteen friars besides the church which was later used as a cathedral. The name, 'Bait Graiza', is in fact derived from the Portuguese 'igrezia', meaning a church.

Few people living in Oman now walk the old path used in the time of the Portuguese over the mountains to Matrah. It is an interesting but exhausting walk taking about two and a half hours and definitely not to be attempted in the hot season. The track runs roughly from the wadi beyond the British Bank of the Middle East to the end of the old runway at Bait al Falaj, but both locations have changed so drastically in the last few years that it is doubtful if even the old-timers could find the path now.

Until 1973 there were two landmarks in Matrah – the Bab al Kabir, the old City Gate, and the Charles Knox Memorial Hospital, better known as the Mission Hospital. In February 1973, the Bab al Kabir – shattered no doubt by the sudden onrush of motor traffic shaking its foundations to the very core – suddenly gave up the ghost one Friday and collapsed in a pile of rubble injuring three people. As it was Friday the area was almost deserted. Had it been a weekday there would undoubtedly have been a death toll.

The gate, which dated back to the seventeenth century and was thought to have been built by the Portuguese, was situated in an area which had once been the terminus for the chief caravan routes of south-east Arabia, but since 1970 it had been used as a taxi-rank. Today no-one would know there had ever been a gate there at all.

But the other landmark, the Mission Hospital, is still there, much as it has stood for the past forty-odd years, though bits have been added here and there when needed. Now it is called the ArRahma Hospital or Hospital of Compassion, an inspired choice of name by the Sultan which appealed to all who worked there. Seldom can a name have been more apt.

18. The fort at Matrah merges into its rocky background in this view taken from the deck of a visiting ship

The medical work was started in Oman in 1911 by Dr Sharon Thoms, who had formed a close friendship with the young Sayyid Timor who was then in Oman helping his father, Sultan Feisal, carry on the business of government. Sayyid Timor gave Dr Thoms all the encouragement and help he could, even using his influence to help the Mission, the Dutch Reformed Church, purchase the necessary land. Just when all was going well, Dr Thoms was killed in a fall and it was not until 1925 that a replacement, Dr Paul Harrison, could be found. Dr Harrison started work in a rented house on the seashore, Bait Khan, and negotiations for purchase of land for the hospital were restarted – this time successfully.

The hospital was built by the missionaries almost with their bare hands and the forty beds it contained at that time were kept constantly filled. Dr Harrison also found time to do original scientific research and he published several articles in scientific and medical journals on the results of his research in spinal anaesthesia and new techniques for hernia repair.

In 1939, exactly thirty years after his parents arrived in Oman, Dr Wells Thoms, with his wife and family, arrived in Matrah to take the place of Dr Harrison and his wife. There had been a gap of six months between the two doctors and the hospital was empty. World War II had just started, the people of Oman were poor, food and cloth prices were rising – it was a bleak beginning.

Who was to know then what a resounding success the hospital was to become, how the name of Dr Wells Thoms would go down forever in the history of Oman and how, many years later, under a new Sultan, a new Oman was to honour Dr Donald Bosch on behalf of all his colleagues by presenting him with the Order of Oman, the first civilian to hold the honour. It says much for Oman, a strict Moslem country, that one of the first people they honoured under the new regime was a Christian missionary.

If ever there was a tradition of love and service in one family it was in the Thoms family. Sharon, Wells and for a time even son Peter all gave themselves to Oman and its people over a total period of some sixty years. It was Wells Thoms, however, who became nothing less than a legend to his thousands of patients. Specialising in ophthalmology, Wells was responsible for giving back sight to thousand upon thousand of Omanis suffering from the dreaded trachoma, a common enough disease in the country even today.

The most common operation performed in Matrah by far was that for trichiasis, a disease caused by trachoma in which the eyelids turn under and rub against the eyeball, causing great pain and finally blindness. The operation consists of either removing a piece of mucous membrane from the lower lid for a graft or 'taking a tuck' in the eyelid itself, enabling the lid to resume its normal function. I worked in the Mission Hospital myself for three years and have seen Wells perform dozens of these operations in a single afternoon – giving sight to the sightless with as little fuss as he might have bandaged a sprained ankle.

In 1968 when I first started to work at the Mission the conditions were unbelievable to anyone used to hospitals anywhere else. Goats roamed the corridors, even appearing at the theatre door on occasion, people were everywhere – cooking meals in the corridors, their children under foot, or sleeping in odd corners. Patients were often two to a bed and one could seldom be quite sure who was the patient and who the helper for there were no staff to spare for everyday care. Above all, the death toll was high, largely because the patients from the interior had been forced to travel, often for days, over appalling roads where they existed at all, to come for help. To see them arrive was heartbreaking. And all one could do was only such a small drop in such a very large ocean.

In addition to Matrah hospital, Dr Thoms also had to keep an eye on the Muscat Women's hospital, another landmark in Oman whose value to the country has been inestimable. How many healthy young Omani boys and girls and even men and women today owe their lives to the devoted band who worked here so tirelessly day in and day out?

Dr Thoms and his wife Beth and their band of happy followers cared for the people of Oman with an all-encompassing love. In addition to his work in the hospitals, Dr Thoms paid regular visits to towns in the interior and up the Batinah coast, a considerable achievement in those days when the only transport was by camel or donkey. In each town some kind soul would put a building at the disposal of the medical team to act as a dispensary and to this building would come all the sick and injured from the area.

It was difficult not to get embroiled in the local politics of the time. Local Walis made their own laws and often their will was not the will of the people. In addition to being a doctor and a missionary it was often necessary to be something of a diplomat. The Thoms family were all of these things and more, much more. They gave everything to Oman and had the added bonus that the country honoured them for it.

Dr Sharon Thoms is buried in Oman, the country he loved so well, in an unpretentious grave in the Skeikh Jabber cove in Muscat among the foreign seamen and adventurers. Dr Wells Thoms retired to the States in 1970 and died shortly afterwards of cancer. Today the ArRahma Hospital is government-owned and managed though many of the missionaries still work there. It is being improved daily, but the spirit of the missionaries still lingers and the service they gave happily to the suffering still continues in the care given by the young Omani men and women they trained up themselves.

Matrah's pride and joy today is the 'Corniche', a wide double-track road that runs along the seashore where once the fishermen landed their catches in the early morning. It is backed by a line of old and very beautiful houses usually known as the 'Hyderabadi houses', whose backs have now become their fronts, a mixed blessing for the inhabitants but enabling passers by to see the architecture which could once be seen properly only from the sea. Many of these old houses are now topped by radio and television aerials.

Some of the houses are incorporated into the Khoja walled city within a city. Historically a branch of the Shi'ites, the occupants are now Omani citizens and among them are numbered many of Oman's foremost merchants.

Behind the facade is the suq – a maze of semi-covered alleyways where one can buy anything from the latest camera to fresh-ground coffee and halwa made on the spot. The scent of spices is strong here and crowds gather around the second-hand stall. Here are the moneychangers where one can still buy Maria Theresa dollars and there is always the chance that one may pick up a real bargain amongst the old rifles or the tarnished and tinned copper and silverware.

Shouts herald the approach of a coolie carrying a large load straight from a newly arrived dhow or merchantman. The alleys are too narrow and the shopper must vault into the nearest shop, often two feet higher than the alleyway. In the old days spies would be looking for foreign women who showed too much leg when climbing into shops, but those days are past and forgotten, though it is still more comfortable and more practical for women to wear trousers and tunics both for shopping in the suqs and for travelling in the interior.

Where the Corniche now bends its graceful way round the bay of Matrah, where Oman's first pedestrian crossing – a nine-days' wonder – is now taken for granted, is the spot where, before 1970, the dhows from the Batinah coast used to tie up once a week laden with fruit and vegetables. Nowadays they come more prosaically by lorry to unload at the big fruit and vegetable market near to the site of the old gate. Like so much in Oman today, some of the romance has gone, but it is all far more practical.

6. *The Coastline*

The northern coastline of Oman, from Muscat to the border with Fujeira in the United Arab Emirates, is known as the Batinah coast and supports almost one third of the total population of the country. It is largely fertile due to an astonishing number of fresh-water wells, (astonishing because, although in close proximity to the sea, they are untainted by sea water) and provides Oman with the largest part by far of its fresh fruit and vegetables.

Motoring up the Batinah today on the new motorway one could be forgiven for thinking it is extraordinarily dull country. Flat, dusty, the towns, with their ruined forts and dust-covered barasti or palm-frond dwellings, all looking remarkably alike, the whole drive is dull in the extreme. But turn off seawards at almost any point and one is in a different world, a world of date gardens and fruit trees with the constant sound of running water and the calls of birds.

Each of the villages, although harbourless, is noted for its fishermen and has its own fish market close to the sea where the fresh catch is dumped, sold and bought, and put either on trucks or onto donkeys for the last leg into the interior. It is common to see a donkey walking along with what looks like a fishy tail of his own but which is only the trailing cargo lashed across his back. In summer particularly the pair are attended by a very strong and fishy smell and one can only assume that the inhabitants of the interior are possessors of stomachs not addicted to food poisoning like us lesser mortals.

19. The villages of the Batinah, with green palms and rushing water, contrast with their dusty, barren surroundings

The beach which begins at Qurm just beyond the housing area at Ras al Hamra, the first housing area as such in Oman, stretches as far as the eye can see and a lot further, 150 kilometres further all the way up to Sohar in the north. As beaches go, it is quite magnificent. Wide, even at high tide, it is frequented by large crabs and flocks of seabirds and is the happy home of every ornithologist for miles around. It is a world apart – a world of soaring white wings, of sudden splashes, of crabs racing for cover in their hundreds – a wide, wide world of glaring sand and placid bright blue sea, backed up by sand-dunes and distant mountains. Here the osprey sits atop the mast of an old wreck, superior and uninterested. A tern flies out of the blue, dives into the waves with a flurry of spray and emerges, a fish dangling from its mouth. More splashes herald a shoal of sardines darting past and a lone fin slicing the mirror calm indicates a shark on the prowl. Further out to sea tankers float on a glassy sea, suspended in time and motion like figures on a Japanese scroll and the clouds above emerge with the clouds reflected below and life is timeless and infinitely peaceful.

Sometimes it is a wild world of crashing waves and high winds when the shemaal, the wind from the north, hits the coast, but this is unusual.

Boating along the Batinah is probably the nearest anyone could get to paradise. Silently in a sailboat, the wind filling the sails and making the stays whip against the mast, or noisily but speedily in a motor boat, perhaps in company with a shoal of playful dolphins, one can be at one with nature, all the trials and tribulations of everyday life laid aside for the time.

When the tide is out and the sand is firm it is even possible to motor along the beach – a risky business, though, and one that has seen the early demise of several Land Rovers. I nearly lost a Moke that way.

An even greater thrill is to fly along the beach. I once did it in a helicopter at a height of something like six feet. We were actually flying just above the crabs and just under the flocks of birds. It was like having wings of one's own and absolute bliss.

At the Eid al Adha sheep are slaughtered along the beaches of the Batinah and cooked at the same time and the following day the beach is littered with bones, putrid meat, vultures and such a scene of carnage as to turn the toughest stomach.

Travelling north along the Batinah from Qurm, one passes firstly Seeb where Sultan Qaboos has his country palace. One always thinks now of the new International Airport when one hears of Seeb. But long before the airport was thought of – when planes still took off and landed, if they were lucky, at the terrifying old airport of Bait al Falaj or the oil company strip at Azaiba – Seeb was thought of only in connection with gardens, palm trees and running water. It was the nearest 'countryside' to the capital, less than fifty kilometres away from Muscat and those willing to travel by Land Rover over rough and dusty roads could relax there, forget the heat and even swim in the small concrete pools in many of the gardens. There were even – flowers! How many tired businessmen were reminded of the proverb: 'Three things verily of a truth remove care from a man's breast – running water, a green meadow and a comely face'. And many is the comely face along Batinah.

To most of the residents of the capital, of course, even Seeb was out of bounds but the missionaries did have exemption for some reason and every so often we would all go off together in a Land Rover, dressed in our white cotton pantaloons, in a gay end-of-term mood, for a picnic in one of the gardens. We swam with our clothes on (There was no question of being seen in swimsuits) and even the aftermath of wet clammy tunics and trousers was worth the effort. Just before sunset, wet, bedraggled and happy we would jog over the dusty tracks back to Matrah, all singing hymns at the tops of our voices.

Seeb's chief claim to fame goes back to 1920 when the 'Seeb Agreement' was signed between Sultan Taimur, grandfather of the present Sultan, and some of the dissident tribesmen from the interior, led by Issa bin Salih, granting certain measures of autonomy in local affairs to the tribesmen and an amnesty for the rebel leaders in return for keeping the peace. This agreement was broken later by the followers of the Imam when Talib landed rifles and ammunition at Seeb illegally and buried them in the sand for future use.

Forty kilometres further up the coast, past the Government Agricultural Station at Rumais, is Barka. In the middle of the eighteenth century Barka, together with Sohar, was ruled by the Persians and it was here that the last of the Persian garrison were invited by Ahmed bin Said to a great feast to celebrate the departure of the Persian overlords. During the feast Ahmed's men fell on the guests and disarmed them, sending some two hundred of the soldiers onto a ship ostensibly to return them to Persia. The ship caught fire, however, and none but Ahmed's men were saved. The conclusions to be drawn were obvious ones.

Today Barka is a typically sleepy little Batinah village with small farms, some with cattle and sheep, but most growing bananas, dates and figs. One can also find lemons and onions growing and even occasionally grapes.

Passing through the smaller villages of al Musana's and as Suwayq, we come to al Khabura. Each of the villages owes its position to the wadi which opens at that point onto the sea, but al Khabura is at the head of the Wadi Hawasinah, one of the most important and without any doubt one of the most dramatic and picturesque of all the many thousands of wadis in Oman. Leading as it does to Ibri, one of the larger towns in northern Oman, and thence through Wadi Dhank to the Buraimi Oasis, the Wadi Hawasinah has in the past been one of the most important routes into the interior. But even today it is a very rough and steep track. Even Land Rovers have problems and now, of course, it is much easier to travel by the far longer but easier graded road through the Sumail Gap passing Fahud, or the tarmac coast road to Sohar and thence through the Wadi Jizzi to reach Buraimi from Muscat.

Halfway along the Wadi Hawasinah is the Highpoint, a very spectacular point to view the surrounding mountains and the rather hair-raising road one has just travelled or is just about to embark upon.

Passing up the coast through as Saham we come to Sohar. I always have a soft spot for Sohar for it was the one trip I made in the pre-coup days of any length – in those bad old days when we were not allowed to travel at all. It was strictly illegal and I travelled with my sons, all of us dressed in full Arab attire. At Sohar we had our picnic in an old house on the sea front and were getting ready to leave when a thunderous knocking was accompanied by a voice demanding to know if we had permission to be there. We fled. Years later, down in Salalah in South Dhofar, I met the ex-Wali of Sohar who was then standing in for the Wali of Salalah. When I told him my tale he said he remembered the incident well and we had a good laugh about it.

Seeing Sohar today, no-one would believe that once it was a populous and wealthy town described as 'not possible to find on the shore of the Persian Sea nor in all the land of Islam a city more rich in fine buildings and foreign wares'.*

At this time, in the fourth to tenth centuries, Sohar was at its height of prosperity. Peopled largely by seamen and merchants, its importance stemmed from its trade in luxuries and spices between the Far East and India on the one side and the Near East and Europe on the other.

Sohar had a very enviable position for trade. Situated just south of the Straits of Hormuz, it was a natural place for ships from the Gulf to wait for the monsoon when proceeding eastwards to India and the Far East. Here the ships would lay in supplies for the long voyage ahead and on the return journey they would stop first in Sohar before tackling the dangerous passage around the coast of Musandam and through the Straits of Hormuz to the calm waters of the Gulf. The trade from East Africa was also important to Sohar and hides, spices, tortoiseshell and ivory were commonplace in the markets of the town.

Another contributory factor to the town's prosperity was the Wadi Jizzi, which opens its mouth to the sea at Sohar. This wadi, which channelled fresh water to the area, was also one of the most important overland trade routes in Oman, leading as it does direct to Buraimi and thence up to what was once known as the Trucial Coast.

Sohar appears first in records from the first century AD, possibly as a joint capital to the area with Buraimi, but long before this, recent archaeological findings have shown, there were many thousands of burial cairns on the hills behind the town dating back as far as the third millennium.

In the fifth century AD there was a Nestorian bishopric of Mazun (Nestorius, a Syrian prelate, was later banished for heresy). The representatives from Mazun travelled frequently to meetings of the synod in Mesopotamia which accounts for the fact that so much is known of the town over this period.

---

*Istakri in his *Kitab al Masalik wal-Mamalik* composed in the middle of the 4th/10th centuries.

At the time of the Persians Sohar was the seat of the Marzuban, the Persian Governor, and it was here that the first Moslem missionaries landed, meeting the Banu Julanda, then the most important Arab family in Oman.

Shortly after the enforced flight of Mohammed from Mecca to Medina in AD 622, the Persians were driven from the shores of Oman, Sohar falling in AD 629. Eight years later a successful raid was launched from here against the west coast of India. By the fourth century, as we have seen, Sohar was one of the most splendid cities in Islam and boasted a great mosque with a lofty minaret and a beautiful multi-coloured mihrab.

Without doubt Sohar's fame was wide in the Islamic world, this fact being attested to by many writers of the time. Typical of the lyrical descriptions of the town is the following, written by the author of the *Hudd al-Alam*: 'There is no town in the world where merchants are wealthier than here and all the commodities of East, West, South and North are brought to this town and from there carried to different places.'

In its prime, Sohar contained over 12,000 houses, many owned by sea captains, built of bricks, mortar and teak. Dates, bananas and figs grew abundantly and citrus fruit trees from India were introduced into the area by the tenth century. Sohar boasted a cosmopolitan populace of Persians, Syrians, Jews and seamen from as far away as China and India. But of them all the dominant element were the Omani Arabs whose merchants traded with countries as far removed as China and Madagascar.

One of the important features of Sohar was the irrigation system. Watered by fifteen to twenty long aflaj (sing. falaj) which tapped the water sources at the base of the mountains, the area of cultivation at that time was far larger than it is today. Even by the end of the twelfth century it had shrunk to an area not much larger than it is at present.

The fate of Sohar and, indeed, Oman itself, was at that time very dependent on the swing of power in the Near East generally and by the end of the tenth century the Persians were in control of Oman. Years of disorder were to follow and Sohar was never to regain its splendour or its importance. Even so, at the time of the Portuguese, the city still contained some fine houses and the town, dominated by a fortress with six towers, was still described as 'very beautiful'. The fort still stands today, but little of it in its original state. It has had a chequered career, being destroyed and rebuilt many times, and only the north-western tower still resembles its original shape. The fort was in turn under the command of Persians, Portuguese and Omanis, but its greatest moment came when it was the only fort to stand up to the Persian invaders after the fall of Muscat and Matrah in the early eighteenth century. It was at that time under the command of Ahmad Al Bu Sa'id, an ancestor of the ruling family of today.

The town of Sohar today is little more than a sprawling, mud-walled village with palm trees and falaj systems. The fishing boats and shashas, the latter made of sewn and bound palm frond ribs usually about ten feet long with a pointed upcurved bow and stern and a flat bottom, are pulled up on the beach when not at sea and the catch is carried to the nearby fishmarket as it is in all the other villages of the Batinah coast. It is all a long cry from the 'emporium of the whole world' described by the Persian author.

The Batinah, of course, is not the only coastline in Northern Oman. The fine new Corniche road rounding Matrah harbour now continues all the way into Muscat itself, winding its way among the great rocky headlands through delightful little villages such as Kalbuh, once isolated and almost unknown to the casual traveller, while just over the top from Muscat, through a narrow little gap in the hills, is Sedab. Although only a stone's throw from the capital Sedab is surprisingly little known, but it is a beautiful little village with strange round houses and a most attractive coastline.

South of Sedab several pretty little villages, well worth a visit, are now brought within easy reach of the traveller along a spectacular new coastal road which leads from the Ruwi valley, cuts through the hills and follows the coast south to Bandar Jisih. The new road passes through small villages such as Bustan with magnificent sweeping views of the rocky coastline, villages once accessible only by sea or by climbing up and down goat-tracks over the mountains. New villas are springing up in this area today and even hotels – the impact on the villagers is enormous but whether for better or worse only time will tell.

Beyond Bandar Jisih, a beautiful collection of coves, once the favourite weekend haunt for boat owners and ideal for snorkelling (but never quite the same since an Indian ship was beached there after catching fire in Port Qaboos), is Quriyat. As the crow flies, Quriyat is no distance away but one must take the inland road past al Hajjar, an oasis some twenty-five miles south of Muscat and then drive through the Wadi Mijlas to get there. Quriyat is now a sleepy little village, but it has its own niche in history, for in 1814 Qawasimi pirates attacked Sultan Said's forty-gun flagship, the *Caroline*, just off Cape Quriyat and very nearly captured her. It was soon after this that the Qawasim were brought under control, but piracy was always rampant along these shores of Oman.

It was along this coast that, as recently as 1972, thousands of illegal immigrants from Pakistan, lured by promises of good jobs and money by unscrupulous dhow captains, tried to land in the Sultanate. An embarrassment to both governments, they were kept for a time at Bait al Falaj, and finally repatriated by air – all at the expense of the Government of Oman.

Near Quriyat is Siya, where field trips of the Historical Association discovered remains of settlements from the first millennium BC, and evidence of occupation as early as the late fourth or early third millennia BC. Obviously there is much field work waiting here for future archaeologists.

Further south is the larger and better known port of Sur, today linked by a motorway to the capital passing al Kamil, al Qabil on the edge of the Wahhiba sands, and Ibra, a beautiful rambling walled oasis town, comparatively untouched by the frenzy of rebuilding which has hit most other towns of any size in Oman.

The old road to Sur was a narrow track which, after crossing the Sharqiya, ran through an even narrower gateway, the 'Eye of the Needle', down to Bilad Sur, an oasis of date palms, Sunaisalah and then into Sur itself.

Sur is famous for boatbuilding, the dhows (either the bum or the larger baghala) being built in the wide, shallow estuary which cuts the town in half. Across the creek to Aiqa the huris or small motorised boats ferry water and passengers. Aiqa is now a residential area and is like an island with no easy approach from the land. Six ruined forts above the low hills once guarded the approaches from the landward side.

The town of Sur gives an all-over impression of orderliness. The suq and market still retain their old character, but the rest of the town is, on the whole, well laid out and some of the architecture and the old carved doorways are a joy to behold. Along the coast between Sur and Sunaisalah are situated some of the more modern buildings, notably the hospital and the school.

In the early nineteenth century, just inland from Sur, lived a tribe called the Abu Ali. They were the only Omani tribe to become Wahhabis and were consequently distrusted by the other tribes in the country and in particular by the Sultan. A British captain, Perronet Thompson, who came from a strong abolitionist family, was at the time acting as political agent in the area and had been largely responsible for drawing up the treaty which gave its name to the Trucial States, the truce between the British and the pirate chiefs.

While Thompson was in Muscat, before leaving for Bombay, reports came to the Sultan that the Abu Ali were engaged in piracy. Determined to put a stop to this flagrant breach of the law, the Sultan and Thompson between them mustered 2,350 men and landed at Sur, marching inland some sixty miles to administer justice to the tribesmen. When they reached the

20. Designs of dhows have changed little through the centuries. Here a bum unloads cargo at Sur

21. The intricately hand-carved and painted stern of this dhow shows craftsmanship of the highest order

22. Early nineteenth-century hand-carved doors. Those at Sur are among Oman's finest examples

town of Abu Ali which was surrounded by date palms, all appeared quiet, but as they advanced in open column, the British leading, the whole date garden erupted with tribesmen who proceeded to hack the soldiers to pieces. Over 250 men were butchered in the first assault and the remainder of the force fell back to a small fort where they were able to defend themselves. The Sultan had behaved with great bravery, but many of his men had no more stomach for fighting and the survivors straggled back to Muscat where they arrived five days later.

News of the defeat travelled fast and Thompson was blamed for the fiasco: such a defeat involving British troops had never happened before. By January of the following year a new force marched on Abu Ali, this time comprising nearly 3,000 men under the command of Sir Lionel Smith. The Abu Ali fought fiercely, but even they were unable to do battle against the artillery brought to bear on them. Their date gardens and water channels were destroyed and their fort demolished. Hundreds on both sides met their deaths.

Both expeditions were censured by the Court of Directors, but neither commanding officer suffered permanently from the results of their conduct. The Sultan was rid of his enemy, only the Abu Ali did not recover – and there always had been a grave doubt as to whether or not they had indulged in piracy in the first place.

Such is Sur's claim to a niche in history. A sad and ignoble episode and perhaps better to leave buried beneath the blowing sands of the Wahhibas, the sands that appear to advance yearly on the mountains of the Sharqiya. Let us leave it there then and turn our attention to other mountains of Oman, higher, greener and even more dramatic – the mountains of the Jebel Akhdar.

7. The Mountains

Michael Beeching ازکی – جبل أخضر

The Jebel Akhdar, or Green Mountains, that form the whole backbone of Oman are so named because of the greenish colour of the rocks that form them, some of which date back to the Pre-Cambrian era though most of the range is more recent. Here, great towering masses, greenish-tinged like ancient copper, rise sheer to heights of over 3,000 metres and narrow gorges slice their way through them, providing links between villages for men and donkeys but for little else. Small planes, piloted by men with nerves of iron, occasionally fly through Jebel Akhdar rather than over them, thereby reducing their passengers to semi-hysteria.

Because of its inaccessibility, the Jebel Akhdar is not well known to the vast majority of Omanis or travellers passing through, but enthusiastic mountain walkers and climbers with time to spare have taken to spending weekends or even leaves exploring the region and their enthusiasm is contagious. The Army and Air Force, of course, fly up and down regularly, having bases both at the bottom and at the top.

The steep-sided mountains and general terrain of the Jebel Akhdar are perfect for the training of young soldiers and the battle camp up at Saiq, which is centred around a Beau Gestetype fort, is now equipped with eight ranges for the full training of infantry. This means that the men of the Sultan's Armed Forces are now able to train fully all the year round instead of only during the cooler months. The walk up to Saiq, which can take anything from about six hours, is something of an assault course in itself and has been found to be a good way of breaking in new recruits – and Army boots.

Climbing in the Jebel Akhdar can be unpredictable and dangerous for the amateur. During the rainy season, sudden cloudbursts can turn a whole face of vertical limestone cliffs into streaming torrents of waterfalls, often hundreds of metres high, yet at the same time one can never be assured of obtaining fresh water at all and climbers quickly become dehydrated so must carry all their water supplies with them. But all who make the effort find it worth their while for the scenery is wild and exotic and typically Oman.

The Jebel has seen quite a lot of fighting in the past and it was here that the last remnants of the Imam's revolt were flushed out and the rebellion finally quashed. The rebel leader, Sulaiman bin Himyar, was himself caught in a cave near Saiq, a cave which is now one of the local landmarks. Nearby in a wadi bed the remains of a Venom jet are scattered over a wide area of rocks – another reminder of those turbulent days of the 1950s.

But if I have made the mountains sound like one vast rocky wasteland fit only for an assault course, then I have given a wrong impression for the Jebel Akhdar has, in fact, a soft heart – a heart of another sort of green, lush and verdant, full of flowers and rushing water, an area of mud-walled villages clinging precariously to the sides of the mountains with terraces on which the bright green foliage of onions and garlic, the principal crops, stand out vividly against the rocks and where flowers and fruits abound which are almost unknown in the rest of the country. Here it is always pleasantly cool and at night the smell of wood-smoke from the fires fills the air, bringing nostalgia to the traveller and dreams of hill stations in other parts of the world.

Orange groves and vineyards jostle each other for possession of tiny ledges of cultivated soil, inviting pools are fed by rushing water channelled through the age-old falajs as in other parts of Oman, while up and down the boulder-strewn tracks women climb ceaselessly, bunches of wood balanced adroitly on their heads. Flowers are everywhere, especially in spring and early summer, hollyhocks and marigolds particularly growing in a profusion of pink and orange. But it is roses that are the speciality of Saiq and, come the rose season (from about mid-April), roses carpet the hillsides and the villagers occupy themselves making rosewater which they bottle and send down to sell on the plains.

The making of rosewater is done by distillation. The petals and water are boiled in a small bowl or 'sahila' under a larger copper vessel called a 'kurss' which is filled with cool water to help condensation. When the distilled liquid drops down and fills the sahila it is poured into a large pot called a 'burma' and something like a hundred gallons can be produced during one

23. The mountain with date palms clustered around its base, and topped by the remains of a lookout post, is a familiar Omani scene

season. As yet the production of rosewater is very much a cottage industry and most of the little mud-walled huts have their own mud ovens where they light the wood fires to keep the stills going. The bottled rosewater is sent all over Oman, but there is not enough yet to export.

A type of grape juice is also produced from local grapes but, again, the amount is small as yet, barely enough for local consumption.

It is not difficult to visualise Saiq and the neighbouring village of Sharijeh as thriving hill stations of the future surrounded by villas belonging to the wealthier families and possibly offices too for, even with air-conditioning, the output of work in Oman during the scorching summer months is considerably lower than at any other time of the year and, with a good road,

24. Dramatic and sometimes hair-raising tracks in the interior of Oman provide travellers with unique photographic opportunities

commuting to the capital would not be too difficult. But at present villages atop the Jebel are still peaceful and isolated and the villagers as yet uncontaminated by civilisation. The majority of the inhabitants, mostly of the Bani Riyam tribe, work on the land and live in the four main villages, but a few others are pure nomads and, with their mules, spend their lives climbing up and down the precipitous rocky tracks and living in caves. The total population of the whole Jebel area is probably something under 2,000, that is those living on the mountains themselves.

The term Jebel Akhdar means literally 'green mountains', but it has also come to mean the area surrounding them and a large part of interior Oman. The area contains towns like Nizwa, the old capital, Bahla, Jabrine with its famous old fort, Izki (a collection of villages loosely grouped together under one waliyat) Adem, Firq and Birket al Muse. Further away, but still Jebel country rather than Batinah country, are places like Rostaq with its fort and hot springs and al Hazm with another fine and famous fort. Both these forts are imposing edifices, that of Rostaq particularly being more like a walled village than a simple means of defence.

With their great heavy carved and embossed wood doors, their dungeons and old cannon, some even with their own water wells, all the forts of Oman are a source of wonder to the traveller, taking him back in imagination to the past, not so distant in Oman either, when life was hard and simple, when wars were fought with cannon balls and single-shot rifles and often for simple objects like the possession of water wells or the leadership of the tribe.

Cutting through the centre of the Jebel Akhdar country is the Sumail Gap and one of the most remarkable engineering feats in Oman was the construction of an oil pipeline through the gap linking the coast with the interior. When oil was first discovered in sufficient quantities to warrant production, the first thing that had to be done was to build a pipeline to connect the Main Line Pumping Station at Fahud, 270 kilometres into the interior of Oman, with Saih al Maleh, the port where the tankers could load the crude for export. The terrain the pipe had to travel across was the foothills of the Jebel Akhdar.

The pipe was only a part of it: attendant on the line itself were the roads, the camps for the men and, perhaps most important of all, the communications. Nothing existed at all in this part of the country that could help – everything had to be started from scratch. Probably the most remarkable feature of the whole operation was the construction of the five microwave stations linking Fahud with the coast. Built at intervals along the line of the pipe, these stations had of necessity to be at the highest point available, usually at about 6,000 feet above sea level. Some of the locations must at first have looked impossible to the men detailed to build on them. But build on them they did, although often even the special low-range Land Rovers could only get halfway up and the last few thousand feet had to be done on foot, manhandling all the materials necessary for the station.

At the time of the laying of the pipe, Oman was still in a state of unrest. The lorries with their supplies, the ditch diggers, the welding trucks, the wrapping machines, the Land Rovers and, most important, the men themselves all had to be protected from possible attack by rebel tribesmen and in country like that of the Jebel Akhdar this was no easy task. It was a job that fell to

25. Wilbros (Williams Brothers Ltd) trucks carry lengths of pipe on the newly constructed track leading to Fahud, 1966

the Sultan's Armed Forces, a job which they tackled with their usual mixture of enthusiasm and good humour. Indeed a rapport grew up between the soldiers and the 'oily boys' that stood both in good stead for many a year to come.

The pipeline construction was started in 1966 and finished the following year, the first oil for export being pumped through to Saih al Maleh (now called Mina al Falal) in July 1967. By this time there was a graded road along the whole stretch of the pipe and telephonic communication from Fahud to the coast.

No programme of this size would be said to have gone without a hitch, but the numbers of such hitches were remarkably few and the final achievement was a source of pride to everyone connected with it. When the oil started to flow it was indeed the blood that was to bring the corpse of Oman to life.

But the injection of oil into the bloodstream must take its time to reach the extremities. First comes the capital city and the coastal area, for there are the centres of population and the economic centres of the Sultanate today. Soon it will be the turn of the interior – already, indeed, this is well under way. But the extremities will have to wait a little and of these the most out of the way, little known and yet by far the most magnificent, geographically speaking, is the far northern peninsula of Musandam.

8. *The Northern Peninsula*

Belonging to Oman yet separated from her geographically by the United Arab Emirates, Musandam is like a child separated from its mother – and similarly neglected. Little or nothing is known of her past. An expedition from the Royal Geographical Society visited the peninsula in January 1972 and discovered a little but, apart from their findings, Musandam's past is lost in the mists of time.

From the pottery shards which date back as far as 100 BC and the remains of homesteads and what must once have been small villages, the expedition concluded that Musandam must have had some importance, particularly during the time of the Portuguese. In fact, some quality Chinese porcelain discovered at a site near Khasab suggested that the town of that time must have been a fairly flourishing entrepôt on the trading routes from the Far East to the Gulf ports and Europe.

Musandam has always been strategically important, controlling as it does the entrance to the Gulf through the Straits of Hormuz. How much more important today when something like two million tons of shipping passes through the Straits every day, mostly tankers carrying oil from the Gulf to Western Europe and Asia. The Straits of Hormuz are indeed one of the key situations in the world today and the possibility of an imposition of a fixed twelve-mile territorial limit would mean that between them Oman and Iran would control the movement of a large part of the total Arab oil from the Middle East. And Iran is not, of course, an Arab country.

Yet Musandam today is nothing more than an isolated outpost and there are no obvious military or other installations. Once there was a small naval station on Goat Island in the north, but it is now in ruins. The whole peninsula which forms the southern approaches to the Straits is simply a great horn of towering rock, a fantastic world of islands, of wild mountains whose cliffs often fall sheer to the sea for all of their 2,000-odd metres, of deep rocky inlets inaccessible by land and of seas clear as crystal teeming with fish. It is an almost uninhabited world, a veritable Shangri La covering something like 2,000 square kilometres and with a population of under 10,000.

The only way to see Musandam in its context is from the air, for roads as such do not exist other than short rough tracks near one or other of the three villages, the only centres of population in the whole peninsula. It could of course be explored by sea, but it would take a long time and even then the whole could never be appreciated. To fly over Musandam is the experience of a lifetime – groping one's way up unscaleable cliff faces, dropping suddenly over sheer precipices over a thousand metres deep, skimming the emerald waves or flying up a mile-long fjord with towering masses of rock on either side, the peninsula defies description. The traveller, even the normally verbose, is rendered speechless with wonder.

Of the three villages in Musandam only Khasab, the capital of the province could possibly be called a town. The other two – Bukha in the north near the border with Ras al Khaima and Bay'ah in the south near the Fujeira border – are only coastal villages. The three are built where wadis open up to the sea, providing some flat land on which to build or cultivate and there is little room to expand anywhere outside the main settlements except in the area of Khasab. In the entire province only an estimated 400 hectares are under any sort of cultivation.

Yet the visitor comes to the conclusion that here is a place that could easily have a bright future if only as a tourist centre. One of the few really outstanding unspoiled beauty spots left in the world today, the scenery is dramatic in the extreme and a remote island peninsula such as this with its vast rugged fjord-type coastline and its mountains could be a paradise for fishermen, mountaineers, ornithologists and for all those who love the wild places of the world. The small sandy coves at the feet of the craggy mountains would be accessible from the sea and a hotel built on one of the small islands could easily become a holiday centre. The only problem, which is one common to the whole province, would be a shortage of sweet water. The discovery of water could change the whole picture.

26. The only way to appreciate Musandam fully is to view it from the air

Musandam badly needs a trade of its own for it is a province of the very old and the very young, its young people tending to go on up to Dubai and the Gulf area to work, sending their earnings back home in dirhams which is the currency most widely used. None can blame the youngsters for forsaking their homeland for the opportunities at present in Musandam are limited in the extreme. Of those who stay home most are engaged in the fishing industry while others keep goats and sheep or work on the land, mostly growing dates.

But new opportunities are opening up every day. Before 1970 there were no educational or health services in the province at all but today both Khasab and Bukha have schools for boys and girls and at Bay'ah there is a school for boys. An old school at Bukha, built long ago by Abu Dhabi and never used, is now a boarding school for boys from the mountains and from the more inaccessible islands. Education is suddenly popular in Musandam and many of the schools are running on a shift system to make the best possible use of the available buildings and facilities.

On the health side both Khasab and Bay'ah now boast a health centre staffed by doctors and nurses and Bukha has a doctor and a health service with beds for emergencies.

All this is providing work for bright young men and women. But the older inhabitants of Musandam are still conservative in the extreme to the point where, after floods destroyed many of their homes in 1973, they insisted on rebuilding in exactly the same places ready to be washed away by the next flood in spite of pleadings by the police and military.

A squad of the Oman Gendarmerie, a para-military unit of the Sultan's Armed Forces, is based at Khasab, their duties more civil than military and, together with the local Wali, they are responsible for everything that happens in the province from picking up a sick child to stopping illegal immigrants of which Musandam has had its share. Regular patrols are also carried out in the area by the Sultan of Oman's Air Force and patrol boats of the Sultan's Navy visit the area from time to time.

Each of the three villages has its own Wali to keep law and order, but up in the mountains live the Shihuh (The Ichthyophagoi or fish eaters of Ptolemy), a tribe of semi-nomads who are something of a law unto themselves. Speaking a language of their own, Kumzara, the Shihuh can trace their origins back to Persia or Central Asia. Numbers of these tribesmen and women are given as between three and four thousand but this is only a guess and could be way off the mark. The Shihuh build their homes, like eyries, high up on the mountains where they live for a part of the year, coming down to the coast to harvest the date crop. How they get up there or what they live on is a

27. Strange, isolated, mud-walled villages, seemingly uninhabited, provide an intriguing mystery to the traveller in Musandam

complete mystery to the visitor. An isolated and suspicious people, they bury their dead under the floors of their houses as land is so limited, and have in the past used as their chief weapon a short axe-head attached to a long stick with which they kill their enemies by hitting them across the bridge of the nose – a very painful, messy and unpleasant death, one would think.

How much blood-letting still goes on up the mountains is anyone's guess, though it has been said quite recently that blood feuds and tribal wars are still pursued.*

*David Holden in *Farewell to Arabia*.

The inhabitants of Musandam are coming to think of themselves more and more as Omanis though many have never even heard of Muscat and are inclined to think of Sultan Qaboos as their own personal Sultan. Oman in turn is developing a greater responsibility towards her lost child though the separation factor does not help. Musandam, in fact, is still something of a problem, but then problem children often turn out to be the most brilliant and already the possibilities are there, for a French

28. High in the mountains of Musandam, a Shihuh village perches precariously above the jagged coastline

company which was awarded an offshore concession in 1973 is drilling for oil, though so far without success. Musandam will just have to be patient.

Certainly Musandam gives Oman little trouble, unlike her other problem child in the far South, also separated but not by sea or even by other powers but by 700 miles of desert.

9. The Southern Province

South Dhofar has been a part of Oman since the last part of the nineteenth century although it has always had close connections with the Hadhramaut. It is something of a mystical province. For nearly half the year it is enveloped in the mists of the monsoon which affect the rest of the country not at all, and its history also goes back into the mists – of time. Dhofar indeed is said to have been the Ophir of Biblical times and as early as 1,000 BC traders shipped frankincense from Dhofar to the markets of Egypt and Assyria. The 'Quinquiremes of Nineveh from distant Ophir'* with their cargoes of Sandalwood and cedarwood no doubt had a considerable amount of Frankincense aboard as well.

Frankincense – the very word has a magic about it. The three Kings with their gifts to baby Jesus – gold, frankincense and myrrh – the Song of Solomon and the hills of frankincense, the incense used by the Romans. Dhofar was the chief source of this heaven-sent commodity.

*John Masefield: 'Cargoes'.

How can we appreciate it today when perfume is commonplace and when cleanliness is indeed next to Godliness if not at times ahead of it? Yet in those far-off days frankincense was not a luxury but a necessity to disguise other and less pleasant odours, to perfume clothes, to give as a gift, to work and often to die for. Because supplies were limited, it also had a scarcity value and became at times almost priceless. The 'Frankincense Route', leading from the production area in Dhofar northwards to the markets in Assyria and Egypt was jealously guarded and the jewel drops of fragrant gum from the trees of Arabia were lauded and hoarded, written about and sung about and well-nigh worshipped.

As far back as April 1952, American Foundation archaeologists who had been working with little success at Ras Raysut, west of Salalah, turned their attentions to some rather uninteresting looking ruins at Khor Rori, near present-day Taqa. The first day of digging revealed coins and an inscribed tablet, the forerunners of finds that were to prove the ruins to be that of the ancient fortress of Sumhuram (Samaram) which once guarded the frankincense port of Moscha. It was from this port that the frankincense was shipped to the Hadhrami port of Cana for transhipment to the outside world and, together with the 'Frankincense Route' north ensured supplies to the surrounding areas at all times of the year. More recently much valuable work on Sumhuram and Moscha was done by the late Mr Andrew Williamson of the Dept of Antiquities, who was tragically killed while exploring the area, also by a French team (see *Journal of Oman Studies*, vol. I, 1975) and by A. F. L. Beeston the following year (*Journal of Oman Studies*, vol. II).

Different areas produce different varieties of incense, the best being the 'silver frankincense' from behind the Qara mountains, the lowest quality that nearest the sea. Most of the gathering of the incense is done by the Bait Kathir tribe who predominate in the growing area and in the old days only certain families had the honour of gathering the fragrant droplets. Almost aseptic conditions were demanded, uncontaminated incense being used in conjunction with prayer to secure immortality. For frankincense was not only a prized commodity, it had an almost religious significance. It was also a very vital part of the burial ceremony, largely one suspects because it disguised the smell of the dead body.

94 Dawn Over Oman

Today the mystique of frankincense is largely gone but the gum resin is still gathered in season and can still be bought in the suqs of Salalah. From March until August, the stunted bushes are tapped like rubber trees and the latex, in hard droplets, almost without odour until warmed, is left to dry in the sun. Roll a droplet of frankincense in the palm of your hand, shut your eyes and smell – then you may get an inkling of what it was all about. Yet the bush is very unpretentious, stunted and bare and no visitor would look twice unless he knew it for what it was.

It is a sad fact that Dhofar has become known more for its war than for its incense over the past years, a war which, as we have seen, lasted some thirteen years – a war of rebels, camel trains of arms and death from the air. Sadly, it was a completely unnecessary war for after 1970 at least, there was never any reason

29. A frankincense bush in South Dhofar, the unexpected source of a priceless commodity

behind the so-called 'rebel cause' and no reason why Dhofar should not have been sharing all along in the national prosperity. However, now the war is over, Oman is making it up to her unfortunate offspring and, per capita, the Southern Province has lately been doing better out of the newly acquired oil wealth than anywhere else in Oman. The focus is more and more on Dhofar and to emphasise this even the National Celebrations in 1977 were held in Salalah rather than in Muscat.

Even while the war was still on, new buildings and improvements on the coastal plain flourished under an enthusiastic and imaginative Dhofar Development Board and now the good work can be continued up into the Jebel area, which until recently was largely enemy-held. In the last stages of the war, as areas became 'white' (rebel-free) CATs (Civil Action Teams) moved in behind the army. These CATs comprised a medic, a schoolteacher and a storekeeper and together they helped villagers to start new lives, giving them hope for the future where there had been none.

Now that peace has come to the Jebel the great agricultural plans which have been hamstrung for so long can go full steam ahead. The Jebalis have always been cattle farmers, their cattle being small, wiry and tough. During the war the Ministry of Agriculture and Fisheries carried out a great number of experiments on the breeding and feeding of cattle on the plains. An Animal Breeding Centre at Bir Bint Ahmed, a 72-hectare farm for fattening bull calves at Garzaiz as well as livestock, poultry and veterinary centres were staffed by experts from overseas and Omani trainees to find the best breed to suit the Omani climate and terrain. Cattle were brought in from overseas to breed with the local cattle in order to establish a type ideal for the climate and for fattening into beef cattle.

Not all the experiments were a success of course. The first cattle to arrive in Oman were far too large for breeding and consumed far too much fodder which also had to be imported. Eventually, however, cattle from Kenya, smaller and more akin to Jebali cattle, were imported with great success and many were sent up into the Jebel to run with the herds even while the war was still on. In time it is hoped to export beef in considerable quantities to Northern Oman and even the Gulf area. Dairy produce, too, has proved a great success and a local co-operative has been established for some years to market vegetables and fruit produced in the area. Today, far from being the liability it was in the past, Dhofar is becoming one of Oman's greatest assets.

During the war, it was a strange experience to visit Dhofar – all development on the one hand and, on the other, all the fear, misery and bloodshed of a country at war. At times, the two were drawn together and the poor wretched innocents dragged into the maelstrom must have felt a schizophrenic sense of hopelessness.

When one talks of Dhofar today one usually means South Dhofar – the Qara mountains and the coastal plain on which stands Salalah, the provincial capital (In point of fact the Qara mountains are only the central range, the coastal range being called the Jebel al Qamar, the range to the east the Jebel Samhan and the northern Jebel towards the Jazir in South Oman and Jebel Zaulaul.) There is, of course, North Dhofar, the Nejd, where the mountains slope more gradually to the thousands of square kilometres of desert which itself fades imperceptibly across the sand-dunes into the infinite wastes of the Rub al Khali, the Empty Quarter.

Other than oilmen, few give this part of Oman a second thought and the only centres of population are small villages grouped around water wells, villages like Marmul, Mowaffaq, Khasfa, Dauka and Fasad. The only population of any size is around Thamarit, or Midway as it is more commonly called, now a hive of industry and known best for the 'Midway Road', a road through the Qara Mountains leading down to the Salalah and the only land link between the coastal plain and Northern Oman. This road was closed for most of the war years but is now one of the great arteries of the country.

The geography of Dhofar is quite unique. First the coast where, near to the border with the People's Democratic Republic of Yemen, mountains of one to one and a half thousand metres fall sheer to the sea. Further east the coastal plain opens up, green and arable, with coconut palms abounding. Here is Salalah, the very heart of Dhofar – one could almost say the heart of all Oman. Water here is plentiful all the year round, though during the war many of the falajs were cut or blocked by the rebels, thereby cutting off the supply to the plain. Today the falajs are working again, bringing fresh sweet water from the mountains to irrigate the plain – an essential ingredient to the new agricultural policy of the province, a legacy of the past contributing to the prosperity of the future.

Behind the plain is the Jebel itself, rising to heights of over two thousand metres. Both historically and traditionally the Jebel is a separate area from the plain and its people, the Jebalis, are smaller, wirier and generally more alert than their counterparts on the plain, the majority of whom are descended from slaves imported from East Africa by previous sultans.

The Jebali men, mainly cattle breeders, have long, curly hair bound with a leather cord called a mahfif. They dress in a short, skirt-like garment with a blanket thrown over their shoulders and have a native lively intelligence and a quick wit. Because of this they were the Omanis who, under the reign of Sultan Said bin Timur, outwardly rebelled. Many got away to places like Saudia Arabia and Kuwait where they obtained education and, on their return, were able to see how wrong things were in their own country. It was up here in the Jebel that the Dhofar Liberation Front was established with its main aim the overthrow of Sultan Said. But complications arose. In 1967 the British withdrew from Aden and by the end of 1968 the Communist influence had grown alarmingly. By the end of 1969 the Front had changed and had become Communist-dominated. No longer was it the Dhofar Liberation Front but the Popular Front for the Liberation of Oman and the Arabian Gulf.

Then came July 1970 and the overthrow of the Sultan. Now the real root cause of the original rebellion had been removed once and for all and a new young sultan was installed full of ideas for the modernisation of his country. But it was not to be that easy to give up and return to the fold, for the Communists had their teeth well into the trousers of Oman and a little thing like this was not going to make them let go.

Now the terrorism began, terrorism that Communists have perfected all over the world in places like Malaya, Vietnam and in hundreds of less well-known areas. The Jebalis began to live lives of fear, torn between loyalties, their families always at risk. Over the years they have seen their fathers, husbands and brothers killed and tortured; the men have seen their womenfolk raped and parents have had their young sons kidnapped and sent across the border to be trained in the art of warfare at Hauf in PDRY. Even when they began to realise what the Communist doctrine was all about they were bound in fear to help their erstwhile comrades. And the 'comrades' were coming in a different guise: no longer were they the fatherly, brotherly men, anxious to help and promote their doctrine in a stealthy way. The new 'comrades' were highly trained specialists, arrogant, fearless and cruel, with a first loyalty to Chairman Mao.

Towards the end of the war the Chinese influence had largely given way to the Russian, and hardline Arab countries such as Libya and Iraq had become involved. Without outside help it is doubtful whether Oman could have kept the pack at bay but by this time Iran, Jordan, and to a lesser extent Saudi Arabia and the Gulf States had realised that Oman's fight was also theirs. Contributions to Oman's war effort snowballed and by the end of 1975 the war was declared officially over. Thousands of tribesmen, mostly brought up to Muscat by lorry on the newly-opened Midway Road, gathered in the police stadium at Qurm to celebrate the occasion with a great show of singing, dancing and patriotic speeches. They deserved their victory and a great time was had by all.

There were still problems of course. While the war was still on, many hundreds of rebels had surrendered to the Government forces, the numbers increasing as the war drew to its close. Many of these SEPs (Surrendered Enemy Personnel) were recruited into the Firqa Units (Home Guard) with promises of land and jobs when the war was over, promises not always easy or expedient to keep.

As we have seen, the war provided an excellent training ground for troops from Oman itself and from friendly countries such as Britain, and later Iran and Jordan who sent help in kind. Aircraft always played a vital role, particularly helicopters, and I can remember several rather hair-raising trips over the Jebel during the war, particularly once when we tried to land at the forward post of Simba (Sarfait as it was called in official communiques) during a heavy enemy attack. With me in the plane were the COSOAF, the Brigade Major, a Flight Lieutenant and five goats in plastic bags being taken to the front for fresh meat (the goats that is). I was more worried about the goats than the enemy for if they had decided to run amok there was no telling what might have happened. In the event we were not able to land at all but flew back to Manston, another forward post, to have lunch in an underground mess complete with Persian carpets and, more to the point, cold beer.

Flying up to the Jebel posts in those days was a somewhat terrifying experience for the layman, even without the enemy, as it was necessary to lose height as quickly as possible to minimise the chances of being hit by enemy fire. The noise of the rotors combined with the dizzying fall down the barren rocky Jebel and the clouds of dust at the critical moment of landing made one only too glad to fall to the ground and run for it.

Simba covered an area of some twelve square kilometres. The airstrip on 'Mainbrace' was protected by artillery on 'Yardarm' and each platoon was so well dug in that they could withstand

30. A unit of Firqa (Home Guard) troops on reconnaissance, following tracks of the 'adu', or enemy. This picture was taken in the final stages of the Dhofar War

even a direct hit from the enemy mortars. Casualties to the Government troops were therefore minimal yet the casualties they could inflict on the enemy were considerable. Simba was a strong, natural position and, even in the worst days, remained impregnable.

Flying over Simba, the biggest surprise was the nearness of Hauf, only after all some twelve kilometres away across the border in PDRY. Hauf had always been the base camp for the rebels – more, for it incorporated a Revolutionary Training Camp once shot up in a particularly daring attack by the Sultan of Oman's Air Force as a reprisal for a rebel attack on the fort of Habrut north of the Jebel and in Omani territory.

One must of course bear in mind that borders in this part of the world are anything but definite. In 1966 a border commission was established to set out once and for all the correct borders between the Aden Protectorate as it was then and Oman. Politically it was not a difficult exercise as the British were, so to speak, on both sides and it became largely a matter for the British Foreign Office. The border was finally established to everyone's satisfaction when Sultan Said bin Timur, on a cruise along the Dhofar coast, suddenly spotted a particular rock and shouted out 'Ah, there is the split rock, there is my border'. Since the split rock was some four kilometres to the east of where the border commission had drawn their line, everyone was slightly nonplussed. No-one seems to remember the outcome.

One thing is sure in this area: Simba is Oman and Hauf is PDRY. That no one could dispute. There have, however, been several border incidents started by rebels who, by accident or design, have shelled positions in Omani territory. Oman, apart from taking the obvious course of complaining to the Arab League and the United Nations, has usually managed to give back better than she got and the incidents then died a natural death.

The final victory in Dhofar was brought about largely by a policy of establishing lines of posts controlling the routes through the wadis north of Mughsayl, thirty-five kilometres to the west of Salalah, to behind the Qara mountains. When the posts finally linked together, the Hornbeam Line, they successfully prevented all but a trickle of enemy supplies from getting through to the east.

It was a war that could have continued indefinitely, the terrain being very much on the side of the 'adu' or enemy for even quite large camel trains loaded with supplies and arms were able to hide out under the overhang of rocks at the first approach of the Sultan's Air Force while the periodic mists allowed them to creep in and fire on the plain. As jet aircraft of SOAF soared down over the odd camel it must sometimes have seemed to the pilots much like taking a hammer to kill an ant.

While the victory was most certainly a military one, other factors were involved in the latter years, largely on the diplomatic side, which no doubt contributed to the final solution. But the war has not ended for the Jebalis overnight and it will take several years for the situation to return to complete normality, up in the mountains at least.

But the Jebalis, of course, comprise only about fifteen per cent of the total population of Dhofar province which is given as

31. Gaily dressed women of Salalah on their way to market. Many people in Salalah are descended from negroes imported as slaves for the royal household

between twenty-five and fifty thousand. Over eighty per cent live on the plain and in the towns of Taqa and Marbat and life on the plain was always surprisingly normal considering how close the war was. Even in the bad days men still worked on the land, harvested coconuts, caught fish and bred cattle. In the suqs of Salalah merchants sold their wares while spies from the adu mingled with soldiers of the Sultan's forces and Firqas and Jebalis from the mountains shopped alongside Western contractors.

Today there is a new spirit abroad and change is everywhere: tarmac roads, new blocks of shops and offices, new villas and hospitals and everywhere projects and yet more projects. Even the old Palace, once the home of a thousand rumours, where the old Sultan was chased up and down the corridors and finally captured, and where the new Sultan took office such a very short time ago, has had such a facelift as to be almost unrecognisable.

The surf still thunders on the beach as it always did but the predominating sound now is that of the hammers of the workmen.

PART 3

10. *Natural History*

Petroleum Development (Oman) Ltd, Oman's first petroleum-producing company took as its symbol the oryx, which it duly represented on its company flag. The flag has not been seen much lately, which is not altogether surprising for it has come to their notice that the oryx is almost on the point of extinction in Oman, if not already extinct.

The Arabian oryx appears to have two names in Oman – Al Bakr al Wahsh, or wild cow, or the more common Bin Sola or son of violence, which name is also said to belong to an antelope with large antlers found on the Jebel Akhdar. Certainly the oryx is no son of violence, but the name of Bin Sola is that commonly used by the tribes bordering the Empty Quarter which is the last area in which oryx have been seen in Oman.

The oryx is a type of antelope with two rapier-like horns which, seen from the side, can look like one, giving rise to the belief that the oryx was the original unicorn. It has been hunted in the past for food as well as for sport and the Bedu girls are alleged to have made flutes from its horns. It is a handsome animal, white with brown and black markings and at one time it ranged over the entire Arabian peninsula and northwards as far as Palestine and Syria. Today, the odd oryx is a rarity and reports of an oryx seen in Oman are acted upon at once for Sultan Qaboos is keen to preserve the species if it is at all possible.

The haunt of the oryx is, or was, along the western borders of Oman, a border unpatrolled and unmarked, and it is difficult if not impossible to keep track of the hunting parties in this part of the country for frontiers exist only on paper and a party can run down and kill an oryx on Omani territory and be away across the frontier before anything is known, if indeed it ever is.

In the early 1970s a conservationist and wildlife photographer friend of mine working in Oman spent two weeks living with a group of Harasis and following tracks of what were believed to be the last live herd of wild oryx in Oman. By the sheerest misfortune, the party was preceded by two parties of illegal hunters travelling in two Land Rovers who, only days before the Harasis reached the scene, chased, captured and killed five oryx, most probably the only ones living in a wild state in the whole of Arabia. It was a tragedy that would have gone unnoticed and was discovered just too late to make any difference.

Superstitions regarding the oryx do not help for they give the horns and stomach juices aphrodisiac powers and the belief is prevalent that killing an oryx bestows on the hunter the strength and stamina of the animal killed. Balanced against these beliefs are the high prices now being paid for live oryx. One can appreciate the hunters dilemma!

The total number of oryx in the world today is almost certainly under two hundred, probably considerably less. There are herds in captivity in the United States and small captive herds in Riyadh, Qatar and Abu Dhabi, one of which was recently the victim of a fatal disease. It would seem that the days of the wild oryx, in Arabia at least, are numbered.

This disappearance of the oryx in Arabia is well-known and deplored by environmentalists but a species of mountain goat, the tahr, has only in the last five years been causing the same concern. The Arabian tahr (*Hiuitraqus jayakari*) is a particularly beautiful type of wild goat with two short curved horns sweeping back from the top of his head and with a white stripe along its muzzle. The species found in the Jebel Akhdar is not to be found anywhere else in the world. Two other types of tahr are found in the Nilgiris in Southern India and in the Himalayas and Dr David Harrison, the world's leading authority on Arabian mammals, presumes that the tahr entered Oman by a former landbridge connecting this country to Southern Persia and once

32. A captive oryx, plump and well fed. The two rapier-like horns when seen from the side can look like a single horn, and this may have given rise to the unicorn legend

there evolved as a separate species quite different from its Asian cousins.

In 1973, Dr Harrison and the Fauna Preservation Society of London suggested a mission into the interior of Oman to locate the tahr and find a likely place for a game reserve. The Sultan himself became so interested in the idea that, in 1974, he set up an Office for the Preservation and Development of the Environment in Muscat to act as an advisory body to the Government in all matters affecting the flora, fauna and environment generally of Oman. Both the World Wildlife Fund and the International Union of Conservation of Natural Resources co-operated with the Oman Government in financing a two-year project for the particular study and preservation of the Arabian tahr, some fifty of which are believed to roam the cliffs of the Jebel Aswad in Northern Oman.

In April 1975, a team consisting of experts in botany, mammalogy, ornithology, reptiles, entomology and with a professional photographer came to Oman and spent a month collecting specimens in all their separate fields and taking photographs. Two new species were discovered by the team, a new species of bat – *Eptesicus bottae omanensis* – and a new species of carob tree. The team also recommended that an area in either the Jebel Akhdar or Jebel Aswad should be preserved as a National Park. As a direct result of the team's recommendations a reserve has been set up on the Jebel Aswad and twelve local tribesmen have been recruited as rangers. Just as important, Oman has now introduced laws forbidding the shooting of the tahr, the ibex and the white oryx, which has the Sultan's special protection.

I have never seen any of these animals myself in Oman though I have seen a gazelle in the wild state in the Hajjar Basin. It is a most beautiful sight, a creature of the wild in his natural habitat, and it is difficult to understand how man could bring himself to shoot one, at least for pleasure. But where there is beauty there will always be someone to desecrate it.

When I hear of men shooting gazelles I am always reminded of a friend of mine, a Libyan, who went on a shooting party in a Land Rover across the Sahara. They chased a particular gazelle for miles across the rocky wastes before catching up with it and shooting it. 'When I looked at it with its great black eyes full of tears,' he told me, 'I wanted to be sick, and I never hunted again.' I hope other hunters feel this way, but I very much doubt it. Yet in Arabian folklore the gazelle often changes into a beautiful girl and vice versa. Perhaps this is a point the hunters might bear in mind.

Gazelle are comparatively common in Oman, but it is unusual to find them outside the stony deserts which they prefer to the sand. Many are cared for as pets – and very attractive pets they make. In spite of their fragile appearance they are quite tough little animals and soon learn to live with humans. I once saw a small gazelle standing beside the airstrip at Heima in southern Oman. The Fokker Friendship was making the most terrible noise prior to take-off and churning up clouds of yellow sand, but the gazelle, obviously a pet of the Seismic Camp, was standing placidly watching and not batting either of his beautiful eyelids.

Perhaps the most astonishing thing about gazelles is the speed at which they move. On tiny, spidery thin legs they seem to fly across the stony desert, desert that would soon break a man's ankle if he tried to run across the same ground.

The casual traveller across Oman's deserts will probably come away with the idea that fauna here are almost non-existent but such is far from the case. One need only spend a night camping in the sand-dunes where game tracks are obvious to realise the following morning just how much animal life has passed by in the previous night, animals unseen and unsuspected. Where rain is unknown game tracks just go on accumulating and it is said that in some parts of the Empty Quarter there are tracks still visible after more than a thousand years.

Among the most common desert animals seen, or usually not seen, are wolves, badgers, hares, hedgehogs, foxes, gazelles and thubs. Thubs, or spine-tailed monitors, are a kind of lizard which prefer the stony desert to the sand. They can grow to a length of about three feet and are eaten by the Bedu who stew them, probably out of necessity for they must be as tough as the proverbial old boots. To all these tracks can be added those of common lizards, scorpions and varieties of snakes and the smaller beetles, spiders and other insects – the desert is no place for the squeamish. Omanis believe, incidentally, that if you see a snake and let it go, it will come for you and get you the next day, but this I have proved false.

Other mammals said to inhabit the sandy desert but never actually seen recently are the wahl and the rim, a large white gazelle. Reports of cheetah and leopard have also come down the years, particularly in the Qara mountains in Dhofar, but recent sightings of all these animals have yet to be substantiated.

Oman now also forbids the shooting of the hubara bustard. This magnificent bird, once common along the Batinah, is now on the world list of endangered species. The hunting of birds generally on the coast is also prohibited.

Bird-watching in Oman is a very rewarding pastime for it is on the crossroads of the migrations and this geographical location, coupled with the climate and the abundance of food and vegetation particularly along the coast, makes the area a paradise for bird-watchers for many months of the year. The autumn migration usually occurs in Oman from August to October while the spring passage may last from February through to April, and during these months many hundreds of exotic species can be seen along the Batinah coast.

Even apart from the migrants, Oman has a good number of attractive habitats. Ospreys are common residents along the shores as are terns, sooty gulls and the occasional flamingoes. Marshes and lagoons are the favourite habitat of the long-legged herons. The two-colour phases, black and white, of the reef herons are the most common while the slightly larger grey heron is a less common variety. Little bitterns and little green herons breed in the thick mangrove swamps.

The waders are among the best represented birds in Oman from the tiny sand plovers that scuttle along the beach at the waves' edge to the graceful long-legged black-winged stilt. Crab plovers with their distinctive cackling call are unique to Arabian shores and in Oman young birds may be seen in September when they breed along deserted tracks of beach.

Inland, in the date gardens of the Batinah, purple sunbirds, like iridescent purple and black jewels, flit between the flowers, sucking out the nectar with their long curved beaks. Brilliant coloured bee eaters are also common, while the magnificent roller takes flight on azure blue wings, providing an extra splash of colour among the green palms.

Further inland on the gravel plains and on the foothills of the mountains, wheatears (both humes chat and desert) can be seen. Rock thrushes and Egyptian vultures are a common sight. Egyptian vultures are indeed among the most common birds in Oman – one can become quite attached to them although I personally never get used to the idea of one flying over my car, his shadow on the bonnet, as they are prone to do. It does not do to be superstitious. But no-one, surely, could become attached to the griffon vulture, usually seen atop the carcass of a camel, his long stringy neck tucked well into the more tempting putrified organs until he jerks it back suddenly, something unspeakable in his mouth and an evil look in his eye.

Higher into the mountains eagles and falcons dominate the bird life. Short-toed eagles and bonellis eagles have been found nesting in almost inaccessible crags while peregrine, saker and lanner falcons can be seen high up over the mountains stalking their prey and swooping down into the wadis, blending with the scenery to the extent that the eye can seldom follow their progress.

Further into the deserts and bordering the Empty Quarter the desert larks and cream-coloured coursers have their home, but the Arabian ostrich which was once widespread in this area has been extinct since 1941.

Of the migrants, eagles, hawks and buzzards that breed in Asia Minor pass southwards to Africa, while waders breeding as far north as Siberia may winter in the area. The autumn migration is especially good for waders while the spring passage seems more to bring in the passerines or perching birds.

Better known even than the birds of Oman are the fish, for Oman's seas generally teem with fish, though there have been bad years which have been put down by various experts as due to cold currents, plankton, oil or even the whims of Poseidon. The most common fish is the sardine which travels in shoals of thousands close to the surface where they are easily caught by trawling nets between boats. They can be seen coming, often quite close to shore, and it is amusing to watch a bunch of fishermen apparently resting on the beach, to hear a sudden yell and watch fascinated while they gather up their 'dish-dashes' (the long white cotton garment worn by almost every man in Oman regardless of his job in life or his station) and run for the boats. Only minutes later they return with sagging nets and much laughter.

112 *Dawn Over Oman*

Larger fish which are quite common in Oman include the sail fish, the king fish, barracuda and varieties of shark. All these are found close to shore and I once saw three fourteen-foot hammerhead sharks laid out on the beach at Seeb where they had been caught within a few yards of the shore. More exotic specimens from deeper waters are the porpoises or dolphins, tuna, parrot fish, Portuguese men o'war (a rather lethal jelly fish) and the sea snakes. Also common in Oman waters are turtles and

33. Harvest of the sea. Sharks (on the left a hammerhead) among the early-morning catch at Matrah.

during the right season, from November to May, they come up on the beaches in their hundreds to lay their eggs. To watch this ritual is an unforgettable experience. We once spent a night on the beach just south of Ras al Hadd, the most easterly point of the Arabian peninsula, and soon after sunset we spotted strange red pinpoints of light along the beach. To our astonishment these turned out to be the reflection of the moon in the eyes of hundreds of turtles coming up out of the sea like primeval monsters on a predestined course. We spent the whole night with the turtles and saw the whole process from the first flying sand the mother turtle scoops out to make her lying-in bed to the last track in the sand as the turtles return to the sea, their ordeal over. As an added bonus we watched baby turtles from a previous laying scurrying for the sea and helped them on their way. Normally most of the eggs and nearly all the babies would have been eaten by foxes during the night or by gulls during daylight but that night we increased the odds of survival considerably.

It has been said that turtles are afraid of man but that night this was certainly not the case. The mother turtles even seemed to welcome company during their confinements and one could imagine the babies were only too glad of a helping hand to the sea. I have even seen a turtle swimming in Muscat harbour just ahead of the royal yacht, the *Al Said*.

And this bring us, inevitably, to another favourite Oman hobby – shell collecting. From the small boy clutching his first few shells off the beach to the learned conchologist poring over his latest *Cypria pulchra*, the joy and wonder of shell collecting knows no bounds for even the humblest shell is surely a work of art. In Oman there are something like four to five hundred species readily available. Of cowries, probably the most beautiful of all, there are thirteen types to be found in Oman, eight of them quite common, while cones, volutes and the spiny murex are also easily attainable.

Oman has a unique advantage when it comes to shell collecting for she boasts not only the long sandy beaches of the Batinah, but areas of rocks and coral so that both types of molluscs are commonplace.

Those too lazy to forage for themselves can always go to the suq and buy a 'five finger' or *Lambis truncata sebae*, the large, spiky shell up to one foot long or the *Bursa bubo* which used to have its end knocked off to be used as a very effective horn, much as a conch is used in other parts of the world.

One of the world's leading conchologists, Dr Donald Bosch, has lived in Oman for many years and not only possesses an unrivalled collection of shells from the area but has discovered

34. Three types of shell discovered in Oman by Dr Donald Bosch. Left to right: Acteon eloiseae Abbott, Conus boschi Clover and Cymatium boschi

no less than three new species, the *Cymatium boschi*, the *Camus boschi* and the *Acteon eloiseae*. So the serious-minded collector always has the chance, be it ever so slim, of finding a new species and putting his name to it for posterity.

But of all the shells in Oman none, surely, could rival the cowrie with its exotic colour and brilliant sheen. Cowrie shells must be collected when they are still alive and the animal taken out by one of a variety of unpleasant ways to preserve their natural lustre, after which the shell must be kept out of the light as much as possible. But it is well worthwhile for a box of cowrie shells is as beautiful and sometimes as rare as any case full of jewels.

11. Arts and Crafts

The arts and crafts of Oman are far from sophisticated and centre around the making of silver jewellery and coffee pots and the embellishment of rifles.

The jewellery of Oman has a certain barbaric charm – chunky, asymmetrical and rough – and collectors can have a wonderful time scouring the suqs and spotting possible bargains among the silver and copper, not always an easy job as much of the lovely old copper has been tinned over and can only be restored with a power drill, a hard but very rewarding task. The women of Oman, even those in the humblest villages, are decked in silver from head to toe and even quite small girls are often loaded down with silver jewellery and ornaments.

The suqs of Oman were until comparatively recently filled with silver. It is hardly surprising that in the last few years so much has disappeared for nearly every foreigner who has ever lived in Oman has his private collection of Khanjars, coffee-pots, bracelets and rings and many other people, who should have known better, even took to carrying silver out in bulk for resale overseas. It is still possible, however, to get most of these items with a word in the right quarter but prices have soared and few people are willing to pay the sort of money demanded.

Enthusiasts, both Omani and foreign, have attempted to stem the flood of the really good antiques destined for homes abroad, although sadly much has already departed never to return. But there is an excellent broad-based collection in the Museum at Qurm, and one can only hope that not too much has got through the net.

Shopping in Oman has all the excitement of the chase. As an example, some years ago a shopper browsing round the Matrah suq found a particularly handsome rifle. On close examination he found it bore a plaque which read: 'Presented by Chester A. Arthur, President of the United States, to Seyud Toorkee Bin Seyud Sultan of Muscat in token of friendship.' Sultan Turki Bin Said was a great-great-grandfather of the present Sultan of Oman and the rifle, which was late nineteenth century, was valued at £750 sterling. Fortunately for Oman the shopper who discovered the rifle immediately presented it to the Museum after getting it cleaned professionally by another enthusiast who also made a suitable display case.

Not every shopper can hope for such luck but bargains abound, particularly if the buyer has any knowledge at all of the subject. Even the universal Maria Theresa dollar, which is still used as currency in parts of the interior, can be a bargain if one knows which date to look for. The large silver Maria Theresa dollar should surely be classed as a financial wonder of the world. First struck in 1751 in Vienna and destined purely for the Austrian market, the 'thaler' soon became a coin for universal trading and ten years after the first one was issued in Austria it had found its way to the shores of Arabia. It has never looked back. Not only are these coins still used for trading in Oman today but they are also frequently used as adornment. Singly, strung on chains, or many adorning a necklace, the variations are endless.

One might well ask why a coin from a now comparatively obscure European country should still be in demand half a world away. The answer is that the coin over the years has maintained its value, stabilised its weight and is as secure as any gold bar or silver ingot. What matters that it bears the head of a female ruler of the now defunct Austro-Hungarian Empire? When it changes hands in the suqs of Oman, no-one would look twice or quibble about the exchange rate. And who cares about Maria Theresa herself? Not many it seems, for more often than not the silver jewellery in Oman has been obtained from the melted down thaler which is always to hand and much easier to acquire than the imported silver ingots which are shipped in from India and Pakistan.

The vast majority of Maria Theresa dollars are dated 1780, the date of the lady's death. Any other dates than this are worth looking out for.

The centre of the silver craftsmen is the old capital city of Nizwa. Here, under the shadow of the vast circular fort, silver workers and merchants sit behind their stalls in the covered ways surrounded by every kind of jewellery and every size of coffee pot. Where a shaft of sunlight breaks its way through the barasti roofs, the silver dazzles the shopper whose eyes have got accustomed to the darkness of the alleyways. The tourist is already dazzled by choice – between nose rings, earrings, toe rings and rings especially made for each of the four fingers. The only real problem is how much one can afford to spend.

Designs are simple in the extreme – basic geometrical patterns, simplified Arabic writing, stylised flowers, often called the 'rose of Nizwa' design, and the lucky 'hand of Fatimah', Fatimah being the daughter of the prophet.

Another draw for the shopper is the rifle, ornamented with silver and embellished with designs and often with Arabic script. The two most common rifles offered for sale in Oman are the matchlock and the Martini. The matchlock is an ancient type of musket or arquebus (so named because of the method of support during firing) and the explorer Sir Richard Burton, who was once attacked by Bedu carrying these muskets, commented on the wisps of smoke seen rising from the match which often prevented an effective ambush. Powder, ball and wadding are rammed down the barrel and the powder measured into a little cup near the touch hole. This usually has a sliding cap which to some extent stops it getting wet and falling out. The match is made of material soaked in saltpetre (found in bat droppings) wrapped around the stock and the smouldering end held in a serpentine or metal clip linked to a strangely shaped trigger. The curved stock is then held against the shoulder in under the armpit and the trigger is pressed. The smouldering match should then come into contact with the powder in the pan and firing takes place. It sounds, and is, a very complicated and haphazard method of firing and one cannot help wondering how many tribesmen over the years have blown themselves up rather than those they were firing at.

But the weapons are treasured now for their beauty rather than for their effectiveness and can often be works of art with their silver facings and bindings of copper and brass. The barrel is usually attached to the stock by rawhide which shrinks to a tight fit, and tucked into the coiled match is a metal or wooden snuffer and sometimes a container jar for keeping the match alight and out of the way.

The Martini is a much more modern rifle and is still used today, being carried slung under the arm parallel with the ground. It is a simple breech-loader and comes in several designs with long or short barrels of differing calibres and varying in the amount of silver decoration.

Most of the Martinis were manufactured in the 1870s and 1880s and the ammunition is still easy to obtain though unreliable. To reload the empty cases they must first be hammered through a set of swages to give them the correct size for the chamber. The .22 cap is then filled with three match-heads and a piece of sandpaper, the case filled roughly with homemade gunpowder and the soft blunt lead bullet wedged into it. The whole is then given a polish with dust and loomi (lime) skin and sold.

A friend of mine in the Sultan's Armed Forces told me that the original Boxer rounds can still be seen occasionally and are quite rare and valuable today. They have wound brass cases and paper patches round the bullet and they are, he assured me, 'great fun to fire for the first pull of the trigger seldom gets them off but when they do go there is a very satisfactory boom and lots of smoke'. This weapon is similar to the ones used by the British Army in the film *Zulu*, a great favourite with the Sultan's Forces in Oman, which has been shown innumerable times and is always sure of a vast audience.

Rifles and jewellery apart there are other strange objects whose function is often in doubt, among foreigners at least. A

35. An Omani hurss, containing verses from the Koran, with lucky pendants

'kohl container' with an applicator with which ladies darken their eyelids and lashes has puzzled many a shopper and an argument still rages in Muscat today over the purpose of some strange silver objects thought by many to be hair curlers, although others contend they are extra large ear-rings.

Another favourite buy is the 'hurss', the small silver box worn round the neck in which is carried selected verses from the Koran. These can be anything from simple, plain little boxes to large and very ornamental ones the size of a wallet with dangling silver pieces attached. My own favourite pieces of jewellery are the very rough silver discs on which is written a verse from the Koran. The disc is worn on a chain round the neck – an amulet and a talking point as well as an unusual piece of decoration.

Omani coffee pots follow a traditional pattern and many are highly prized by collectors, from the old copper pot bought in the suq and polished lovingly over the years to the magnificent specimen presented to the United Nations by the Oman Government. Many so-called coffee pots, incidentally, are not coffee pots at all but water containers, brought around after a meal by a servant while another carries a bowl. The guest is expected to hold out his hands while the water carrier pours water over them into the bowl: he is then given a small towel on which to dry them.

To digress for a moment, etiquette is as important in Oman as it is anywhere else in the Arab world. Guests are expected to remove their shoes, to tuck their feet under them when they sit on the floor (it is considered impolite to show the soles of the feet), to partake of three cups of coffee (no more no less) and to go through many rituals of speech refusing but eventually accepting the place of honour and so on. Although the number of stylised phrases, of honorifics and greetings often seems excessive to the foreign guest, it is also a great help to those whose Arabic is not sufficient to maintain a long conversation. It is also as well to think of one's own language deficiencies – the incessant conversations regarding weather in northern climes for example, or the prevalence in the English language of the 'you know' used even by those whose education has been of the best.

To return to the silver, the most beautiful of all Omani silver is without doubt the khanjar, the ornamental dagger worn by all male Omanis and the symbol of the country itself. Every visitor

36. A traditional Omani silver coffee pot from Nizwa

37. A silver khanjar. The special shape of its handle shows that it belongs to a member of the ruling family

to the country covets a khanjar and one is limited only by the price one is willing to pay, for the supply is endless. Although khanjars are beautiful pieces of art work with blades which can be sharpened to a fine point, I had never thought of them as serious weapons, due to the difficulty of getting them out of their sheaths in a hurry. I asked the Sultan himself about this once but he told me this was not so – and proved his point very effectively!

Allied to the weapons of war are the hide shields made, it is said, from rhinoceros hide from East Africa. These are not made now, of course, but provide interesting and comparatively cheap souvenirs, and many can be found with deep cuts in the hide attesting to their usefulness in the past which all adds to their interest.

There is little embroidery or dressmaking done in Oman other than that for domestic necessity. The most attractive piece of handwork made by the Omani women is probably the embroidered 'kumma', the cap worn by the majority of Omani men. The caps themselves are white and the embroidery brown and it is difficult to obtain a good one as they are made by women for their own menfolk rather than for sale. A few years ago, during a strong shemaal, a very lovely kumma was blown into my back yard. For days I put it out on a stick in the chance that the owner would come and collect it but he never did, so I concluded it was a gift from the Gods and put it with my other souvenirs.

Rugs are made in Oman from goat hair and different colours emanate from different areas. Those from Rostaq are coloured black, gold and maroon while those from Nizwa and Ibri are usually black and white. There are also brightly coloured 'Baluch rugs' – attractive and not too highly priced but not, strictly speaking Omani.

At the village of Firq on the road to Nizwa, dyeing is practised. Leaves are left to soak in large earthenware pots and the dye is boiled over wood fires. The dye is used principally for clothes and is not fast.

Clay pots are made all over the country, usually in simple shapes and the making of earth bricks could also be classed as a craft. Many, too, are the beautiful hand-carved wooden doors throughout the whole country, some of the best I have found being in the town of Sur, south of Muscat.

Dhofar is famous for its pottery incense-burners. Today these are made, not only in the classic square shape but in the forms of aeroplanes, lorries and the like. Not to everyone's taste, true, but very much up to date. Also related to incense are the triangular basket-work stands called 'mabkhara', under which the incense-burner is lit while clothes are draped over it, thus becoming impregnated with perfume.

A rather unusual custom is prevalent in Oman, I am told (though I cannot say it has ever happened to me personally), of lifting up the long skirts of lady visitors and waving the incense burner underneath. The first time I heard of this I did not believe it, but it is apparently true and must come as quite a shock to many visiting ladies, a shock I must admit I would dearly like to witness!

PART 4

.... Rise, my heart, and
Walk with Dawn, for the night has passed.

KAHLIL GIBRAN

38. A young Omani beauty of the new era – with the world at her feet

12. The Dawn Breaks

The speed with which Oman has pulled herself up out of her own Dark Age into the present never ceases to astonish both visitors and residents alike. It is less than ten years now since Sultan Qaboos came to power and everything, it seems, dates back to that time. Comparative figures are always quoted but, to me at least, the whole progress of Oman since July 1970 can be crystallised into the laughing, uncovered faces of the young Omani girls, swinging their school bags and giggling together as girls will. What would have been their lot, one wonders, had things not changed so rapidly for they, for sure, would have been another lost generation. Now they can work and dream – of interesting jobs, of being real wives to their future husbands, of having fine and healthy families. The new buildings are impressive, yes, but what can compare with the future of the young people and the pride in their eyes?

So let us first look at education, the grass-roots of the new Oman. Before 1970 there were but three schools in the whole of Oman, all for boys and catering for something like 900 pupils in toto – and this in a country the approximate size of Italy! There was also a small Mission school for some fifty girls, three small schools for the Hyderabadi community and a technical trade school for the employees of Petroleum Development

Oman Ltd. That was all – a drop in the ocean of ignorance and apathy.

By the middle of 1977, the numbers of schools totalled 261, catering for nearly 65,000 pupils of which over 18,000 were girls. For these youngsters a total of 2,878 teachers had been enrolled, mostly from Egypt, and the schools themselves work on a shift system to get the maximum use out of the buildings and the teachers available. Overseas, many hundreds of students from Oman are now enrolled in foreign universities and special institutes, taking full advantage of the subsidies awarded by the Government.

The old PDO Trade School was taken over by Government in 1971 under the Ministry of Labour & Social Affairs and is today known as the Oman Vocational Training Centre. In addition to the strictly practical curriculum of subjects such as mechanics, motor engineering and electrical installation, pupils are also given a grounding in religious knowledge and languages and the theoretical side of industrial subjects. Many of the students now live on the premises, a great boon to young men from the remoter villages of the interior. There are also Agricultural Schools in Nizwa, a Teachers' Training College at Matrah and basic education centres in Muscat and Sohar. All of these have been financed largely by the World Bank and are supervised by UNESCO.

From northernmost Musandam to southernmost Dhofar, the thirst for education has been insatiable. Children and even adults often walk miles to attend school and teachers without schools and schools without teachers have all been utilised to the full – the very freedom to learn has been intoxicating. The accent has been on primary school teaching – getting the largest number of people to read and write for the first time – and the introduction of broadcasting and various projects developed by the different ministries have added to this training and helped tremendously in the progress of self-education. The Armed Forces, too, have played a part in the education of young soldiers and airmen, not only in the academic field but in the realms of hygiene, sanitation and allied subjects. Many devoted foreigners have given their time and expertise to help the Omanis to stand on their own feet and have opened to them a wider world than they ever knew existed.

The Dawn Breaks   129

It has not been easy at all, for who, in those days of 1970 after the coup, could have decided the priorities in a country where everything was important? It is easy to say education should come first, but what of health, of communication (important, often vital, to other needs), of defence which might mean the difference between having a country to govern or none at all, or of harbour facilities to bring in the essential raw materials for building, and building itself? The list was endless.

Generally speaking, education and health were given the greatest priority after defence had been whittled down to a safe minimum. Setting up a Government Health Service, a monumental task, began in August 1970, at which time there were only three hospitals in the entire country, two run by the American Missionaries and one by PDO, plus a small out-patient

39. Koranic scholars in class. Note the modern-style briefcases, carried as much for status as for utility

annexe to the British Embassy. In the great interior of the country there was nothing other than small clinics or dispensaries run largely by untrained men and women who waged a neverending war on disease and ignorance and must often have wanted to give up the ceaseless struggle. Three years later the hospitals in Oman numbered twelve, served by fifty-four doctors, and there were in addition twenty-five well-equipped clinics. By 1976 hospitals numbered thirteen, clinics and health centres over fifty and there were nearly 170 doctors with over 500 nurses and another 180 assorted Health Assistants, Sanitary Assistants and School Health Visitors. There is still a long way to go in the health field and it will take a generation for young people to learn the full meaning of service to humanity, but Oman has a head start and, granted peace and stability, the road to education and health for all is a bright one.

Peace and stability brings us inevitably to defence. To turn a country into a going concern from scratch would have been difficult enough in a country at peace but for Oman, already engaged in a messy and difficult war in the far south, the problems were increased a hundredfold. The cause for the rebellion may have been removed overnight but, as we have already seen, the Communists were digging in their heels and, far from dying out, the pace was being hotted up by the infiltrators from South Yemen. An increased Army and Air Force was essential – men, supplies, aircraft, the list again was without end – and the money was begrudged by other Government departments who had their own list of priorities. Perhaps if the world had understood the problem, help would have been more forthcoming from other nations whose own security could well have depended on the outcome of the Dhofar War, but there was always a clamp-down on news from the war zone by misguided men who should perhaps have been swept away with the old guard in 1970.

In retrospect, of course, the reasons for the war and the involvement by other nations are better understood. Reasons for secrecy, if they ever existed, have gone and the satisfactory outcome can justify opinions held in the past, right or wrong. However, it is now obvious how much Oman owes to her allies, notably Britain, Iran and Jordan. Most of all, she can be proud of her own armed forces who, by and large, have done a magnificent job under enthusiastic and hard-working officers, often under very difficult conditions. Many of these foreign officers who gave much to Oman and her people over the years with a very real devotion to duty were taunted and haunted by the term 'mercenary'. Indeed, one of the mildest mannered men I ever knew was a mercenary with SAF, and his brother officers' taunts of 'eating babies for breakfast' brought forth nothing over the years but a rather sad smile. Obviously 'mercenaries' come in all shapes and sizes.

The Sultan's Armed Forces, now known as the Sultan of Oman's Land Forces (SOLF), grew in both size and stature over those war-time years which followed the coup and by 1974, as the Dhofar War drew to its close, the Army, once consisting of only three regiments, had seven infantry regiments, an artillery regiment, a signals regiment, a combat engineer unit plus ordnance, mechanical and electrical engineers and medical services. In addition there were seventeen Firqa or Home Guard Units, formed in Dhofar largely from Surrendered Enemy Personel and trained by officers of the regular army. There was even a Pipe and Drum Band – very colourful and very professional. By 1978 SOLF had grown to eight battalions.

By 1974 the Sultan of Oman's Air Force had also grown out of all recognition with four squadrons, one of Strikemaster jets, one support (a Caribou flight plus a Skyvan flight), one of helicopters (Bell 205s and 206s) and a Viscount squadron replaced later by BAC 111s. A fifth squadron of Defenders followed shortly afterwards. Four years later, SOAF comprised a squadron of Jaguars, three transport squadrons, a training squadron of Strikemasters, a helicopter squadron and a Hunter squadron. There was also an integrated air defence system, with two Rapier ground-to-air missile squadrons.

Nor must we forget the Navy, which unfortunately many people do. From a modest 'fleet' of one dhow in 1970, four years later it included the 1,000-ton royal yacht, the *Al Said*, which doubled as a naval patrol vessel, two minesweepers, patrol boats and a fleet auxiliary. In 1978 SON comprised three corvettes, seven fast patrol boats, a coastal freighter, a training ship and other support craft. In addition to fighting the war from the sea down in South Dhofar, the Navy also had to cope with illegal immigrants and fishermen, smuggling and general patrol duty.

A new Naval base was built at Mukallah in Muscat harbour and other smaller bases are either planned or already in use at Bandar Jiseh, just south of Muscat, Raysut in Dhofar and Goat Island in Musandam. The young Omani sailors must be among the proudest in the world.

Pride is no bad thing in a developing nation like Oman and it is a joy to talk with the young soldiers, sailors and airmen and see the light in their eyes at the mention of Sultan Qaboos, the way Oman has progressed and how well they all did down in Dhofar during the days of the war there. Now that the Sultan's forces and their allies have in fact won the war, they can congratulate themselves that they are only the second country since the Second World War (the first being Malaya in the 1950s) actively to oppose Communism in their own country and win decisively. It is quite a thought. More important even than the propaganda value of winning the war is the release of large amounts of revenue for other purposes – for agriculture and fisheries, mineral exploration, encouragement of local arts and crafts and other industries to provide future revenue, for Oman is at present dependent almost entirely on its oil industry which provides well over ninety-five per cent of its entire national income.

PDO is still the only oil-producing company in Oman, though other oil companies are now involved in exploration and drilling. PDO, who started production in Oman first in 1967, now has a Government interest of 60 per cent, the remaining 40 per cent being divided between Shell Petroleum Ltd (85 per cent), Compagnie Français de Petroles (10 per cent) and Participation & Exploration Corporation (5 per cent). In 1968 an offshore concession was awarded to a consortium headed by Wintershall, but no oil was discovered. In February 1973 a concession agreement was signed with a group of four companies, two Canadian, one German and one American (Oman Home Oil Ltd, Cigol Oman Ltd, Deutsch Schachtbau and Tiefbohrgesellschaft Mbh and Oman Sun Oil Co, this last designated as operator for the group). The agreement provided for the exploration of an offshore area south of Masirah Island and covered approximately 13,000 square kilometres. A certain amount of drilling was begun by the Group but so far without success. A French company, ELF/ERAP, has also done some drilling offshore in Musandam but, again, with no results to date.

Oman, although not a member of OPEC, benefits equally and, under the latest agreement, stepped up her participation in the oil industry in Oman to 60 per cent from January 1974.

Allied to the oil industry comes mineral exploration, a source of hope to the Government since Oman has always been associated with minerals of one sort or another. Prospection Ltd and Marshall Oman Exploration Inc, a joint Canadian/American venture, were in 1973 given the rights to prospect in Northern Oman with a special view to locating copper, chromite and nickel. To date copper only has been found in marketable quantities, but hopes still run high.

Both agriculture and fisheries also have high hopes of one day becoming the main prop of the Omani economy after the oil runs down. Before the advent of oil, Omanis earned their living from the land, the principal crops being fruit and vegetables, particularly dates and limes. Generally speaking, Oman has no shortage of water, but it is not easily obtainable and not by any means limitless. Comprehensive surveys of the water resources are continually being undertaken to find new sources and to make the best use of those readily available.

Since 1970 the aim of the Agricultural Department has been more to help the small farmer and his Bedu counterpart to improve on his present methods rather than to try and force new ideas upon him before he is ready. Farming of livestock and rearing of camels, sheep and goats has been encouraged and small farms have sprung up all along the Batinah in the last few years, many now providing fresh produce for the industrial areas north of Muscat.

Before 1970 there were only two very simple Agricultural stations, one at Nizwa and the other at Sohar. These have been taken in hand and improved out of all recognition and in addition other stations have sprung up, notably in the area of Rumais on the Batinah, where continual experiments are conducted to increase the size of already cultivated areas and to introduce new crops. There are also laboratories here and frequent visits by experts from overseas are resulting in greater local expertise everywhere on the agricultural scene.

On the fisheries side, also, a tremendous amount has been done, for in 1970 fishing methods in Oman had altered little for centuries. One of the first tasks, therefore, of the new Government was to set up a Fisheries Department to study and make recommendations on the fishing industry as a whole. In 1971–2 the Government commissioned Mardela International Ltd, an American marine resources development company in association with Del Monte International and FMC International to examine the whole question of fishing, together with the training of local fishermen and the canning, bottling and refrigeration of the catches. In 1973 Mardela brought out the *Darbat*, a small fisheries vessel built in Peru at a cost of some $400,000 and containing all necessary scientific instruments and fishing gear to test the economic potential of fisheries in Oman, both for the domestic and for the export market. The *Darbat* proceeded to ply up and down the coastal waters of Oman searching, teaching and experimenting. By 1975 a detailed report had been submitted to the Government on the recommendations of various experts and on the work done by the *Darbat* itself, which was by now entirely manned by Omanis with the exception of the captain and chief engineer.

One of the main recommendations made by the report was to develop trawling, for foreign trawlers had long been engaged in fishing off the Omani coast, creaming off catches which Oman could ill afford to lose. With proper methods, Mardela suggested that fish catches could be increased up to fifteen times the present total. In addition more exotic fish such as tuna, lobster, oysters and abalone could be a profitable source of future income while seaweed could provide animal feed and fertiliser. Today there is a large ice plant, freezer, cold store and fish processing plant in Matrah and an ice factory in the north near Sohar; others are planned for the future or are already in existence on a smaller scale at intervals along the whole Omani coast.

Expertise is the one thing that is desperately needed in Oman and local expertise rather than that given, however willingly, from abroad. Until the young generation grows up, this will be something of a problem, but when a whole generation comes on the scene, a generation who have been born and bred in Oman and who have benefited from the new regime, many of the present labour problems will be over. There is still some feeling between the Omanis who stayed in the country during the difficult years under the old rule and those who went abroad and came back when Sultan Qaboos came to power. The differences are irreconcilable and the feelings understandable but again, these problems will be solved by the new generations growing up together.

In the meantime Omanis are taking an increasing part in their country's affairs, in particular in the diplomatic and ministerial field which is now almost entirely Omani. It has not been easy for these men, taken from every walk of life and whisked suddenly into the limelight, but the results have been remarkably good and Oman has indeed been fortunate in having so many loyal and enthusiastic men to call upon.

Government in Oman can be considered on two levels – national and regional. The Sultan heads the national government and his appointed ministers are responsible for the various functions of their departments. These ministers bear a collective responsibility for the government of the Sultanate. The regional government follows a more traditional pattern and appointed local Walis govern their own areas. Salalah has its own municipal council, and local government generally is developing into a more sophisticated form all the time. As Oman is now a member of the Arab League and the United Nations, Ministers of State spend much of their working lives abroad. On the diplomatic scene almost forty countries are now represented in the Sultanate and roughly the same number of Omani representatives are in various countries abroad.

It is interesting to note that the most recent exchange of diplomats is with the People's Republic of China. In a television interview after this announcement H. E. Qais Abdulmunem al Zawai, the Minister of State for Foreign Affairs, stated that mutual respect for each other's sovereignty and non-interference in each other's affairs had been spelled out and agreed to by both sides in the establishment of these mutual relations: very useful clauses indeed.

The focal point of all these comings and goings is Seeb International Airport, an airport of very attractive appearance with a runway of over 3,000 metres and room for a future extension capable of taking the largest jets. This airport is now used by all the international airlines operating in the Middle East and gone are the days when airline representatives looked blank when we stated our destination and tried to send us to Moscow for Muscat or Amman for Oman.

On one never-to-be-forgotten day in August 1974, Concorde, then on its hot-weather trials in the Gulf area, landed at Seeb and took about forty of us on a jaunt to Socotra and back as a publicity exercise. A colleague and I, the only women on board, landed back at Seeb in a glorious haze of champagne, caviar and goodwill all round. But our respective husbands hardly spoke to us for a week.

A motorway now links the airport with the Ruwi Valley, where block upon block of flats, offices and shops cover what was once the old runway of Bait al Falaj. I often look up when shopping there and wonder if one day some old-timer piloting his own out-of-date plane will appear over the mountains and attempt to land. He would get a nasty shock, I fear.

Two of the outstanding architectural achievements in the Ruwi Valley today are the Sultan Qaboos Mosque and the Christian Church. The latter was built in the first years after the coup with the blessing of the Sultan himself, and is of an unusual and very functional design. It lacks, however, the character of the little church used previously by the Chrisian community in Muscat. This church was so small that the congregation had of necessity to practise brotherly togetherness, particularly at times like Easter and Christmas. One Christmas Eve I shall always remember. A packed church which flowed out into the outside courtyard and the hushed reverence as three little boys, two Indians and a little British boy, advanced down the aisle dressed as the three wise men swinging their incense burners. When they were halfway down the aisle the dum dum gun went off, splitting the air every few seconds with roars of gunfire (Jalali was only a stone's throw away). At the critical moment the young wise men released the incense, filling the church with smoke, and the lights flickered and went out. A somewhat bewildered congregation never quite knew if we had been bombed or if it was some divine intervention.

The beautiful Sultan Qaboos Mosque, opened in 1977, has become a landmark in the booming Ruwi Valley. Its architecture is very striking, yet simple in its grandeur, and so is in keeping with the Ibadi branch of Islamic faith, to which most Omanis belong. The Mosque is a personal gift from HM Sultan Qaboos, a gift of which the people of the capital area are proud and grateful.

From the Ruwi Valley it is but a kilometre or so to Mina Qaboos, a modern port capable of handling large ocean-going vessels and with a full range of cargo handling and storage facilities. In 1976 the port handled well over a million tons of shipping and the amount is increasing all the time.

Telecommunications, posts, new factories, hotels, the vastly expanded police force and fire services – the list goes on and on.

40. Building development in the Ruwi Valley. Once planes landed and took off at Bait al Falaj airstrip. Now concrete blocks seem to go up overnight

Down in Dhofar another development programme is forging ahead. The harbour at Raysut, by 1974 handling some 250,000 tons of shipping per year, is planned to handle a million tonnes annually by the end of 1978. Raysut is linked by a black-top road to Salalah, and the harbour's main function is to provide a necessary haven for fishermen during the monsoon season. Salalah itself now boasts one of the largest and most modern hospitals in the world while schools, housing developments, shops and power plants seem to spring up overnight. A new runway and terminal building has also taken over from the rather battered airstrip and hutments of the war years.

Low on the list of priorities in Oman in 1970, but in many ways the most important, particularly in Dhofar at war, came the Information Services: radio and, in 1974 television. There is hardly a house today in Muscat, Matrah, Ruwi or Salalah without its television aerial. The first of these services to come to Oman was the radio which arrived with Sultan Qaboos in July 1970 and since then has never looked back. I have a special affection for the radio because two of us, an SAF captain and myself, had the doubtful honour of starting up the first English-speaking service which lasted for some eight months. It was a voluntary assignment and we only went on the air for half an hour a day but it did succeed in driving us both nearly crazy. Anyone who has worked on a small broadcasting station will know the hazards and we were, as I remember, much too ambitious.

The first broadcast I will never forget. Very conscious of the occasion, I started by saying what a great honour and pleasure it was to us to introduce the first English-speaking programme from Oman. I remember then saying, with no qualms at all, 'Now we will go over to the BBC for the world news.' This was followed by a seventeen-second pause (a long time, seventeen seconds) and then a very bored English voice came up reading a share-market report. But we did have our moments of glory.

Radio Oman has flourished over the past eight years. Starting as it did from scratch, it is now widely acclaimed and an indispensable part of the daily lives of the increasing numbers who are able to receive it. It also played a very important part down in Dhofar where the news broadcasts beamed across the border to the People's Democratic Republic of Yemen helped to counteract enemy propaganda from Aden Radio.

Oman television went straight into colour from the word 'go'. Two quite different studios, one for the north and one for the south, have over the last four years provided a good variety of programmes, some imported and some local. The standard of local production is very high and many of these films have been shown overseas.

The whole Information complex in North Oman is gathered together in what is affectionately termed Radio City. This complex was opened in time for the fourth National Day in 1974 and was, in the words of the Sultan, 'a gift to the people'. It has more than justified its existence.

Right at the bottom of the list (but who is to judge its relative importance?) is sport. By the end of 1975 there were over forty sports clubs in Oman under the auspices of a Department of Youth Affairs within the Ministry of Social Affairs and Labour. The accent has been on coaching and already Oman is sending its delegates abroad to participate in international sports events.

Perhaps the crowning glory of the new Oman is the National Stadium at Qurm, opened in a blaze of glory for National Day 1974. The Stadium somehow epitomises the new young Omani – his joy in life, his willingness to take on anyone and his pride in his country. Long may it be so and may he never be disillusioned for, somewhere between the starry-eyed who await miracles and the cynics who have seen it all before lies the reality, and the reality, to my mind is a laughing Omani family with hope for the future and an understandable pride in their country and its recent achievements.

41. Ruler and creator of the new Oman, Sultan Qaboos bin Said, takes the salute at the National Day celebrations, 1974, the last to be held at Bait al Falaj

Bibliography

M. Asraf, *Life of Umar the Great*.

Sir Charles Belgrave, *The Pirate Coast*, London 1966.

Geoffrey Bibby, *Looking for Dilmun*, London 1970.

H. R. P. Dickson, *Arab of the Desert*, London 1949.

David Holden, *Farewell to Arabia*, London 1966.

Journal of Oman Studies, vols I & II.

Life Nature Library, *The Desert*, New York & London 1968.

A Short History of Oman
Hermann F. Eilts, *Ahmad bin Na'Aman's Mission to the US in 1840*
Andrew Williamson, *Sohar and Omani Seafaring in the Indian Ocean*
(all produced and published by Petroleum Development Oman Ltd).

P.D.O. Annual Reports, 1967–77.

Wendell Phillips, *History of Oman*.
                Unknown Oman, London 1966.

Shell, *The Petroleum Handbook*, London 1966 (5th edn).

Special Report on the Scientific Results of the Oman Flora and Fauna Survey, 1975.

Freya Stark, *The Southern Gates of Arabia*, London 1936.

Wilfred Thesiger, *Arabian Sands*, London 1964.

Index

Abbasid Caliph 12
Abu Ali 74, 77
Abu Dhabi 88
Acteoneloisae 114
Adem 82
Afar 36
agriculture 133
Ahmad Al Bu Sa'id 72
Ahmad bin Sa'id 14, 68
airport 135–6
Akkaddian period 8
Al Bakr al Wahsh *see* oryx
Al Bu Sa'id dynasty 14
Al Haj Ahmad bin Na'man 16
al Hazm 82
Al Khabura 69
Al Musana 69
Al Said 131
Amal 38
ARAMCO 18
ArRahma Hospital (formerly Mission Hospital, Matrah) 60–2
art, rock, *see* rock art
arts and crafts 115–24
asbestos 39
Azaiba 36

Bab al Kabir 59
Badawi, *see* Bedouin
Bahla 82
Bait Ghaliya, Muscat 58
Bait Graiza, Muscat 58, 59
Bait Kathir tribes 41, 93
Bait Nadir, Muscat 58
Balarab bin Sultan 14
Bandar Abbas 15
Bandar Jisih 72
Bani Riyam tribe 82
Banu Julanda 71
Barka 68–9
Batinah coast 65–72
bats 108
Bay'ah 86, 88
Bedouin tribes (Bedu) 12, 41–8, 105, 109; importance of camels to 43–4
Beeston, A. F. L. 93
Ben Naful 21

Bin Sola, *see* oryx
Bir Bint Ahmed 95
birds 110–11
Birka 14
Birket al Muse 82
Bosch, Dr Donald 61, 114
British Petroleum 34, 36
Bukha 86, 88
Buraimi oasis 18–20
Bursa bubo 113–14
Burton, Sir Richard 117

camels 43–4
Camus boschi 114
carob tree 108
Carrington, Lord 55–7
cattle breeding 95
caves 48–9
CFP (Compagnie Français de Pétroles) 34, 36, 132
Charles Knox Memorial Hospital (Mission Hospital) 59, 60–2
Chauncey, Major F. C. L. 22
Cigol Oman Ltd 132
cities 51–64
Cities Service & Richfield 35
Clarke, Christopher 8, 10
coal 39
coastline 65–77
coffee pots 120, *121*
coins 116–17
copper 39, 133
Corniche, Matrah 63, 64
crafts, *see* arts
Cymatium boschi 114

d'Albuquerque, Admiral Alfonso 13
Darbat 134
d'Arcy Exploration Company 34
da Silva, Don Garcia 59
Danka 96
defence 130–2
deserts 41–50
Deutsch Schachtbau und Tiefbohrgesellschaft Mbh 132

Dhofar, South: archaeology of 5–6; geography of 96–7; oil exploration in 38; War of 20–6, 94–5, 97–102
dhows 73, 74, 75
Dilmun (legendary island) 7
Diorite 7
Duru tribes 41, 45; camels of 43
dyeing 123

East India Company 15
education 127–9
embroidery 123
Empty Quarter, see Rub al Khali
Eptesicus bottae omanensis (bat) 108
etiquette 120

Fahud 36
falajs (water channels) 10, *11*, 71, 97
Fasud 96
Firq 82, 123
Firqa Units (Home Guard) 98, *99*, 131
fish 111–13
fisheries 133–4
flints 5–6
Fort Jabrine 14
Fort Mirani 13, 51–3, 54, 59
Fort of Jalali 13, 14, 52, *53*, 54–5
frankincense 92, 93–4

gazelles 108–9
geodes 31
geography, of Oman 29–32
geology 31–2, 34; rock types 32; *see also* oil
Ghaba 36, 38
Ghalib bin Ali 19, 20
Ghubrah 38
Government, of Oman 135
grave-mounds 6–7
Green Mountains, see Jebel Akhdar
gunsmiths 117–18

Habur 38
Hamad 14–15
Harasis tribes 41, 106
Harrison, Dr David 107, 108
Harrison, Dr Paul 61
Harun ar-Rashid 12
Hauf 100
health 129–30
Heima 36
herons 110
history, of Oman 3–17
HMS *Eskimo* 55
HMS *Perseus* 55, *56*
Hospital of Compassion (formerly Mission Hospital, Matrah) 60–2
hubara bustard 110

hurss *119*, 120

Ibadhis 11, 12
ibex 108
Ibri 7, 69
Imam 11, 12
Information Services 138–9
IPC 18, 34–5, 36
Isa bin Salih 17, 68
Islam, origins of 11
Izki 82

Jabrine, fort of 14, 82
Jalali, fort of 13, 14, 52, *53*, 54–5
Janabah tribes 41
Jebalis 26, 95, 97–8, 101
Jebel Akhdar 32, 78–84; War of the 20, *21*
Jebel Aswad 108
jewellery, silver 115–16, *117*

Kalbuh 72
Khanjar 120, *122*, 123
Kharijites 11
Khasab 85, 86, 88
Khasfa 96
Khor Rori 93
Khuzistan 57
kumma 123

Lambis truncata sebae 113
Leninogorsk 57
lizards 109

mabkhara 124
Magan (legendary land) 7
Makan, see Magan
manganese 39
manumission, certificate of 57, *58*
Marbat 102
Mardela International Ltd 134
Mareb 35
Marmul 38, 96
Marshall Oman Exploration Inc. 39, 133
Marzuban 13, 71
matchlock 117
Matrah 1, *24*, 51, 59–64, 128; and work of Mission hospital in, 59, 60–3
Maxwell, Brigadier Colin 5
Mazun (Mezoon) 10, 70
Mina al Falal (formerly Saih al Maleh) 84
Mina Qaboos 137
mineral deposits, exploration of 39–40, 133
mirages 49
Mirani, fort of 13, 51–3, 54, 59
Mission Hospital, Matrah 59, 60–2

Moesgaard Museum of Pre-History, Aarhus, Denmark 6
Moscha 93
mountains 78–84
Mowaffaq 96
Musandam 85–91
Muscat 13, 15, 16, 17, 25, 51–9, 128

Nasir bin Murshid 13
Natih 36, 37
natural gas, exploration of 38
natural history, of Oman 105–14
Near East Development Corporation 34, 36
Nejd 96
Nizwa 20, 21, 82, 117, 128, 133
Northern Peninsula 85–91

OAPEC 39
oil: exploration of, 34–40; formation of 32; pipeline construction 82–4; production of 132–3
Oman Gendarmerie 88
Oman Historical Society 5, 14
Oman Home Oil Ltd 132
Oman Sun Oil Co 132
Oman Vocational Training Centre 128
OPEC 39
oryx 105–6, 107

Partex 35, 36
Participation & Exploration Corporation 132
PDRY 98
Persian conquest, of Oman 10–11
Petroleum Concessions Ltd 34–5
Petroleum Development (Oman) Ltd 35, 36, 38, 39, 132–3
Petroleum Development (Oman & Dhofar) Ltd 35
Phillips, Dr Wendell 35
Portuguese occupation, of Oman 5, 13, 54
pottery 6, 123–4
Prospection Ltd 39, 133

Qaboos bin Said 5, 14, 22, 23, 24, 39, 55, 68, 106, 140
Qaharir 38
Qa'qa 11
Qara Qarat Kibrit 48
Qarat al Milh 48–9
Qarn Alam 38
Qatar 18
Quriyat 72–3

Radio Oman 138–9
Ras al Hamra 36, 67

Ras Raysut 93
Raysut, harbour of 138
Red Adair Company 37
rim 110
Roberts, Edmund 16
rock art 8–10
rosewater 80–1
Rostaq 13, 82
Rub al Khali (Empty Quarter) 96
rugs 123
Ruwi Valley, development of 136–7

Sa'ali cove 57
Said bin Sultan ('Said the Great') 15–17
Said bin Timur 4, 19, 20, 22–3, 24, 35, 55, 56, 97, 100
Saif bin Sultan II 14
Saih al Maleh (Mina al Fahal) 36, 84
Saih Nihayda 38
Saih Rawl 38
Saiq 78–9, 80–1
Salalah 94, 95, 96, 101, 138
salt piercements 48
sand-devils 49
San Joao, *see* Fort of Jalali
sardines 111
Saudi Arabia, and the Buraimi oasis 18–19
Sayyid Abbas bin Feisal 4
Sayyid Timor 61
script, pre-Islamic, in rock art 8–9
Sedab 72
Seeb 68, 135
Shari'a (Moslem law) 11
Sharijeh 81
sharks 112
Sheikh Jabber cove 57, 63
Shell Petroleum Ltd 34, 36, 38, 132
shell collecting 113–14
shemaal 67
shields, hide 123
Shihuh 88–9, 90
silver, ornamental 117, 120, 123
Simba (Sarfait) 98, 99–100
Siya 73
Sleeman, William 16
Smith, Sir Lionel 77
Sohar 12–13, 69–72, 128, 133
Southern Province 92–102; *see also* Dhofar, South
sport 139
Stone Age relics, in South Dhofar 5–6
Straits of Hormuz 85
Sulaiman bin Himyar 79
Sultan bin Saif 13–14, 54
Sultan of Oman's Air Force (SOAF) 131
Sultan of Oman's Land Forces (SOLF) 131
Sultan of Oman's Navy (SON) 131–2

Sultan Qaboos Mosque 136
Sumail Gap 82–4; oil pipeline through 82–4
Sumhuram (Samaram) 93
Sur 73–7

tahr (*Hiuitraqus jayakari*) 106–8
Taimur bin Feisal 17, 34, 68
Talib bin Ali 19, 20, 68
Taqa 102
Thamarit (Midway) 96
Thompson, Perronet 74, 77
Thoms, Dr Sharon 61, 63
Thoms, Dr Wells 61–3
thubs (lizards) 109
trachoma 62
Treaty of Amity & Commerce (1833) 16
tribal structure 12, 41–8
trichiasis 62
Turki Bin Said 116
turtles 112–13

Umm An Nar culture 6

Wadi Aswad 45
Wadi Bani Kharus 8
Wadi Dhank 69
Wadi Hawasinah 69
Wadi Jizzi 70
Wadi Mijlas 73
wadis, rock art of 8–10
Wadi Sahtan 8, *30*
Wadi Sarami *33*
Wadi Uday 8
Wahhabis 17, 18, 74
Wahhiba sands *42*, 43
water channels, *see* falajs
Waters, Richard 16
Williams Brothers Ltd *83*
Williamson, Andrew 93
Women's hospital, Muscat 62
writing, pre-Islamic, in rock art 8–9

Ya'ariba period 14
Yibal 36; 'blow-out' at 37